Everest Trekking With Kids

Adventures to Base Camps in Nepal and Tibet

Neil Mundell

Yeti Books 2nd Printing 2018

Copyright © Neil Mundell
All rights reserved.

ISBN-13: 978-1-9993648-0-9

DEDICATION

Dedicated to Rosie and Freddie

CONTENTS

1	Chapter One - Introduction	2
2	Chapter Two - Everest North Base Camp trek, Tibet	5
3	EBC Tibet – Day 1 Tingri to Lungthang (4300m to 4510m)	11
4	EBC Tibet – Day 2 Lungthang to Lamna La (5150m)	13
5	EBC Tibet – Day 3 Lamna La to Zommug (4790m)	19
6	EBC Tibet – Day 4 Zommug to Rongbuk (4980m)	24
7	EBC Tibet – Day 5 Rongbuk to EBC (5200m)	28
8	The Nepal Earthquake	39
9	Chapter Three – Future Plans	42
10	Chapter Four – Everest Base Camp trek, Nepal Day 1	47
11	EBC Nepal – Day 2 Phakding to Namche Bazar (3440m)	54
12	EBC Nepal – Day 3 Namche Bazar, Acclimatisation day.	61
13	EBC Nepal – Day 4 Namche Bazar to Deboche (3820m)	65
14	EBC Nepal – Day 5 Deboche to Dingboche (4410m)	68
15	EBC Nepal – Day 6 Dingboche, Acclimatisation Day.	74
16	EBC Nepal – Day 7 Dingboche to Lobuche (4940m)	82
17	EBC Nepal – Day 8 Lobuche-Gorak Shep (5164m)	91
18	EBC Nepal – Day 9 Lobuche-Gorak Shep	100
19	EBC Nepal – Days 10 Gorak Shep to EBC (5364m)	102
20	EBC Nepal – Days 11-14 Back to Lukla	116
21	Chapter Five Kathmandu, Camp Hope	126
22	Appendix – Preparation Notes	131
23	About the Author	145

CHAPTER ONE - INTRODUCTION

'That's impossible, it cannot be done'
Ricky Yonzon, experienced trek leader, Nepal, 2016

This book has been written in two stages, initially as a memoir to our Everest trekking trip in 2014 to Tibet, and then after our Everest Base Camp trek in Nepal in 2016. It is dedicated to Rosie and Freddie, who at their current age are still too young to fully realise what they have achieved. Indeed they may not perceive it as unusual, with Rosie saying recently "what's special about going to Everest Base Camp? – it's normal".

As they get older they will start to lose personal memories of their trips, so I have endeavoured to put pen to paper, and a "click to YouTube", in order to preserve some of their remarkable experiences. As time moves on, Tibet and Nepal will too. It may become easier to access areas which are still very remote today. The altitude will be one factor which will never change, so the events noted here will still be impressive many years into the future.

We'd like to thank the many individuals who have called our trips "inspirational" and "amazing". It has become a stark reminder to us that modern day life in the developed world is becoming even more risk-adverse and maybe a little too comfortable to the point that in trying to protect ourselves from external hazards we are inadvertently creating a very unimaginative and unhealthy generation, focused too much on what a small digital screen says rather than experiencing life and this amazing world to the fullest.

As my wife Polly often says to our kids when they ask whether we should walk or drive somewhere, "You've got a pair of legs, so use them". Technology without a doubt makes our life simpler and more convenient, but thank goodness for long summer holidays and the opportunities to remind ourselves of what our bodies are really capable of.

This book also comes with special thanks to Polly for her helpful advice. Much of our travel experiences around the world have been an extension of her own previous travel experiences as a single woman. She is without a doubt the most widely and deeply travelled person I have ever met. Both of us would also like to thank all those at Himalayan Expeditions in Nepal and Tibet who helped make our Everest trips as memorable as they are.

'It always seems impossible until it's done'
— Nelson Mandela

When we discuss our Everest trips with others, my wife Polly and I are struck by the initial disbelief shown by the person listening, and the fact that the achievement rarely registers until we show photographs and spell it out exactly what our children have done. Living in a low-lying area of the UK means we are normally surrounded by a lack of familiarity with high altitude conditions. There is an automatic assumption that because it is unusual, it cannot be done, or as Mt. Everest is involved, it must be too dangerous. People growing up in the UK, being a top-tier and low-lying country, often tend to have a culture of choosing the physically easy option unless competitive sport or self-image is involved. One of the great things about trekking in the third world is that you can have a real adventure, see genuinely different cultures, some we would describe as medieval, and still have a sense of physical achievement.

This book is aimed at the many people around the world who always ask "what can be done" and "could I do that" but need further motivation and evidence that certain physical accomplishments may not be beyond them.

One point to make here is that a trip to Everest Base Camp is what you make it, and also what you expect to get from it. If you turn up expecting 5-star room service and a Costa coffee shop in every village you are going to be disappointed. Doing some basic research into trek length, weather conditions, AMS (Altitude Mountain Sickness) and being very well prepared physically, and having good and relevant outdoor kit will make it the trip of a lifetime.

We do have one specific health warning, we advise that altitude related illnesses be taken seriously with high altitude trekking. We recommend trekkers refer to documents on the British Mountaineering Council website (www.thebmc.co.uk). Before attempting to take kids to both Tibet and Nepal, we spent a lot of time researching the causes and effects of AMS (Altitude Mountain Sickness) and feel that it is part of our duty of care to bring attention to these as part of this text.

CHAPTER TWO – EVEREST NORTH BASE CAMP TREK, TIBET

This following text details our experiences in trekking to Everest Base Camp (EBC) in Tibet, prior to the Nepalese earthquake of 2015. We trekked as a family including our 6 year-old son and 7 year-old daughter. Both kids became amongst the youngest people to trek to either of the Everest Base Camps, and perhaps the youngest to do it in Tibet. The achievement was not recognized by the Guinness Book of Records when we made the claim in 2015, as they were too young and GWR only recognize records involving the summit. For interest, our searches show at the time we arrived at EBC in Tibet, the previous youngest record holders include an 8 year-old American, followed by a 7 year-old Indian boy, both to EBC on the Nepalese side. In December 2014, several months after our trip, a 5-year-old Indian boy claimed the record, again on the Nepalese side. We could not find any information on children previously trekking to EBC in Tibet.

Introduction

In August 2014 we set off on a tour of Lhasa and surrounding areas in preparation for the trek of a lifetime, 70km at high altitude over 5 days, with our kids aged 6 and 7, to the Tibetan North Everest Base Camp.

Since birth Rosie and Freddie have accompanied us on global travels and are no strangers to long haul flights. Previous adventures for them have included Rajasthan and Northern India, south-west China, Xian, Beijing, as well as a couple of touring trips to Hawaii and North America. Indeed, Freddie took his first steps on a beach in Maui, and at 3 was walking in the Haleakala volcano area at around 10,000 ft. Polly, my wife, is a true global traveller. Before having kids, she spent every school holiday escaping the huge pile of English Literature homework marking to explore and trek in the remote Himalayas, Asia and further afield in South America and Africa. She has many stories to tell from having a tiger "eat" her pupil's homework in India to accidentally falling asleep against the Dali-Lama, and unwittingly marrying a sheath-wearing Amazonian warrior! Since becoming a mum she has been eager to put her rucksack back on and continue exploring. She is acutely aware of cultural nuances of many remote civilizations. I distinctly remember local female sheikhs making a beeline for her when we visited the Golden Temple in Amritsar. Wherever we go in the third world, she often finds herself at the centre of attention, drawing crowds of curious locals, whereas other Westerners on the other hand tend to be treated with indifference. Polly's experience as a teacher and interest in local people often draws attention. Our first media attention was in India at the Golden Temple when local photographers reported on the 'young family' touring Rajasthan – we were clearly not following the normal tourist route. Perhaps we stood out as we sat and interacted with locals during prayers in the temple, while other tourists, typically with no children, would only observe from a distance.

One thing we have eventually come to realise, is that travelling with kids as a family unit opens many doors when it comes to interacting with local communities within less developed nations – indeed the family unit is the cornerstone of communities the world over.

I am on the other hand, a fairly straightforward oil and gas explorer, and a budding ex-army officer hopeful, with that career option removed by dodgy tendons at Sandhurst. My uni days were dominated by me pursuing ever more endorphin-satisfying fitness feats, such as running 10 miles some mornings with a 40 lb backpack. Working offshore at the start of my career, 2 week onshore breaks gave me some opportunity to walk in the Scottish mountains. Later in my career I moved to London, and the eventual need to return to the mountains pushed me to joining a trekking trip to Ecuador, to climb Cotopaxi. This is where I met Polly. It would take another few years after having two kids, bar some ski trips to Lake Louise and the Alps, before we were ready to start tackling some hills more seriously.

During the kids very early years, Polly insisted that they walk everywhere she walked, by the age of 3 they both thought nothing of walking from our house in Surbiton to Kingston and back on shopping trips, 5-6 miles if not quite a bit more. In preparation for the Everest trip later, day walks along the Dorset coastline, around Buttermere, Catbells and nine hour days at Snowdon from the age of 4 to 5 meant the kids were well adjusted to walking in the outdoors. We spent the summer of 2013 in southwest China's Yunnan province, where Polly organized some long fairly high altitude day walks in the Jade Dragon Snow Mountains near Lijiang and Shangri-La. Culturally resembling Tibet, this was a sensible test of the kids openness to longer walking trips.

One concern with Himalaya trekking is reaction to altitude, with the commonly quoted "1 in 4 suffering" spelt almost certain trouble for our family unit. Both Polly and I together have witnessed many reactions to altitude, and I myself have suffered and recovered to know the symptoms. Prior to Tibet we tried to get medical advice relating to altitude effects in children, with very little success. Polly, who usually takes the lead in planning our trips, sensibly allowed 2-3 weeks prior to the Everest trek in walking at gradually increasing altitude to ensure we had the best possible preparation. Polly also had one major issue herself to overcome - just 6 months earlier she underwent spinal surgery to remove part of a protruding disc. Less than a year before our trip to Tibet she was worried about not being able to walk for any significant distance again. She wanted to do this trip in 2014 to motivate herself to recover, despite me asking her to wait until 2015 once she knew she had indeed fully recovered. However, as fate would show, a 2015 trip would not have happened with the Nepal earthquake affecting Tibet as well. I have no doubt the earthquake would have caused us to be more cautious and not organize an independent trip at that time.

Upon arrival in Lhasa, following a couple of days in Kathmandu, the kids and I immediately felt the effects of altitude (3650m). It felt like the hangover from hell, with paracetamol not having a huge effect. My previous altitude related illness was at over 4800m, so I was surprised to feel the symptoms at this lower altitude. Walking at a slightly fast pace caused a shortness of breath - you could see why aerosol cans of oxygen are widely available in local shops. The effects wore off after a day or two, and the next couple of weeks gave us the opportunity to gradually improve our fitness by training our bodies to function in thinner and thinner air. Polly planned our Tibetan trip very carefully, to include several day trips to monasteries at gradually higher altitudes in and around Lhasa, as well as enroute to the start of the trek. The two week cultural trip cleverly provided plenty of opportunity to acclimatise prior to the trek itself.

The EBC trek in Tibet starts at the village of Tingri. Unlike the Nepalese trek, it is possible by drive by 4x4 for much of the way. As we were to find out, that is the easy but unadventurous way, guaranteed to miss much enroute (and with a very bumpy road not that enjoyable I would suggest). Our trekking company, based in Colorado, had subcontracted a Nepalese company who then subcontracted a local Tibetan company to organise our trek. The tents were dry and comfortable and the food was very basic and Tibetan (not good), but we were given a dedicated guide to take us to EBC. This was roughing it by Western and Nepalese standards, almost to the point where we managed the trip despite the provisions given. We would have been better off with a gas stove and tins of baked beans every day. On arrival at the first campsite we played some football, with our guide trying to ensure that Freddie and I did not run, as he was concerned that we were still acclimatizing to the altitude. Indeed running did have an impact, with both myself and Freddie stopping after half an hour or so due to tiredness. We retired for the night before our trek started in the morning.

EBC TIBET - DAY 1

Tingri to Lungthang (4300m to 4510m)

After our first trial sleep in the tents, we set off. The day was dry and hot with the green flat pastures in front of us leading to the start of the mountain range. Our local guide Dobbla walked with us the entire way. After a few hours the first signs of fatigue would start to appear, with my legs feeling the strain already. The land was quite flat and barren. Despite the guide saying he had done the walk many times, he became "navigationally embarrassed" as he tried to locate our lunch stop, where the other staff were waiting for us. The day wore on in sweltering heat, we were starting to wonder if we had enough water for the day. After perhaps 8 hours of walking we finally found the correct valley to walk up, to where the village of Lungthang is located, with our campsite already set up. Both Rosie and Freddie were in good spirits, with Freddie walking a lot with Dobbla, who had taken a shine to him. Our 6-8 hour day had turned into 10-12 by the time our guide had his bearings. I was slightly concerned by his lack of map and compass, good boots, survival bag or temporary shelter to shield us from the sun, but was reassured that he had done this many times. He was certainly fit enough to be a professional guide. This day was a slog, walking across barren flat pastures, through marsh in desert-like heat to the foothills of the Himalayan mountain range. I thought to myself "at least it's uphill from here" so good for fitness training.

Rosie and Freddie both did well and enjoyed a game of football in the evening.

Campsite at the end of Day 1. We camped at the base of the foothills, where the days ahead would see us climb into higher elevations.

EBC TIBET – DAY 2

Lungthang to Lamna La (5150m)

This day had a difficult start to it. It was uphill along dirt-tracks from the village. Freddie threw his first tantrum but was soon cheered up by some sweets and the guide's good sense of fun with him. The route we took started on a very long not-so-gentle incline for a couple of miles before meandering long left and right turns before we entered the valley system, searching for the correct route.

I recall stopping after a couple of hours, with an Australian group driving back from EBC, with jaws on the ground in awe of the fact we were walking with 2 young kids.

"That's amazing; good for you". We carried on for an hour or two parallel to the next set of foothills before entering the valley leading to Lamna La Pass. The valley was stunning with wide vistas and a long climb up and back down to the valley floor, where we stopped by a river for a break. Lots of Chinese tourists started waving and asking where we were from, and couldn't believe what we were attempting. We carried on up and up through the valley for what seemed an eternity. Both kids were happy to go with the flow; I think they were enjoying it.

Rosie with a sun-kissed dad. The sun at high altitude is very strong and apparently also affects dress-sense.

Entering the valley towards the Lamna La Pass - wide open vistas made this a spectacular walk.

We reached the top of the Lamna La Pass in late afternoon, at which point we only had a couple of hours walking left to the campsite. Again a 6-hour day had turned into a 10-12 hour day. At the top of the Lamna La Pass I thought to myself "At least it's downhill from here" so good for resting knackered legs. At the campsite a couple of hours later I was thinking 'this is a bloody nightmare' but with the kids present I verbalised the sentiment as "You're doing well Rosie and Freddie, we'll soon be there". I recalled some of the infantry exercises I had done with the regular army in Canada some 20 years earlier, and this seemed much tougher. I had been nominated ("volunteered") as the family packhorse, so throughout the day I was handed more and more items to carry. I may as well have had a sticker on my head "If you can't be arsed carrying it, give it to Daddy - it'll be good for his fitness training".

Spectacular rolling hills make this part of the trek incredibly scenic.

The day was very long, sunny and dry. The type where you need a cold beer and a barbeque. Not here though, the camp food was very basic but at least they had coffee. There wasn't much time to rest before dark here. Typically on this trek, we would arrive at the campsite around an hour before nightfall. With young kids present the time was used intensely to sort out the kids sleeping bags and clothes for the next day. We had very little time to reflect on how each day had gone.

Our guide and Freddie walk ahead making good progress.

EBC TIBET – DAY 3

Lamna La to Zommug (4790m)

Today was all about uphill to the pass with long vistas at the top of the mountain range. Again, whilst trekking at altitude, it makes a difference to acclimatisation if you "walk high, sleep low". The downside is that every morning is faced with a muscle-warming morale-challenging slope to contend with. As a group, morale was kept high. To date the weather was dry which helped, but that was all about to change. After a few hours walking on the sweeping pastures on top of the pass, the skies darkened. The speed of the weather change was impressive, we were at the very top of the pass at 5300m, higher than EBC itself. Thunder started to crack literally and what seemed immediately above our heads - we were after all above most weather systems back home. Polly told the guide that we needed to find shelter, I told the kids to put on their waterproofs. Within a couple of minutes we were being battered by lashing hailstones and heavy rainfall. Lightning was striking the ground nearby and thunder was drumming in the skies all around us. Rosie and Freddie were scared, so we rushed along the path to a village about a kilometer away. Thunder continued to break around us with the dark skies occasionally broken with flashes of streak lightning.

Polly and Dobbla paused and looked at me, with rain

pouring around us.

"Sir, are you OK?" Dobbla asked. Apparently lightning had struck the ground within a couple of feet just behind me. Since I had my back to it I hadn't realised what had happened. Polly had helpfully said a few minutes earlier "we need to get off this mountain top, we don't want to be the tallest thing around". Well, Dobbla was quite short as is Polly, and the kids were 6 and 7, making me the tallest object for lightning to hit. I knew there was a reason for me being there - a decoy for electric bolts. Since meeting Polly I have nearly been hit by lightning twice, firstly in Cambodia in 2005, where a bolt struck just five feet directly in front of me, halfway between myself and a local fisherman giving us a lift along the Mekong. That bolt was so close I could measure it, about one to two feet wide I reckon. Today's bolt was directly behind me, closer perhaps. I have joked with Polly that I should take out lightning insurance, or make a bet that I'll be hit by lightning sometime in August in the next few years!

We rushed to the nearby village, soaking wet despite our new "Gore-Tex Pro" mountain jackets. The disadvantage of good waterproofs is that the water runs down the front of the jacket onto your trousers, potentially giving the local villagers the unusual perception that all Westerners have major bladder control issues. On reaching the village our guide invited us into one of the local family houses, where we were welcomed with the warm Tibetan hospitality.

The house was very basic, with twenty or so family members or local villagers sitting in the main room, all clearly escaping the storm outside. There was silence when we entered; they clearly had no interactions previously with outsiders, and couldn't speak a single word of English – or at least they were being very cautious with us. When we travel with young kids, the ice is normally broken by the female head of the local family, relating her own experience with children. One of the older ladies spoke to Dobbla and asked if we would like some tea. In Tibet, this typically means the local speciality of Yak-butter tea.

Not specifically aiming to be culturally insensitive, but there is a reason why Yak-butter tea hasn't made it to the dizzy heights of the shelves of Waitrose in Surbiton. To make Yak-butter tea using western ingredients do the following - buy a pint of milk, leave it opened (not in the fridge) for around 10 days, add 50g of butter and half a kilo of salt. Stir and heat until it resembles a drink. Then sip and spit out, remembering to smile and hope no-one notices. Local delicacies stay local for a reason. Being "head" of the family, I also served the purpose of the being the formal recipient of local hospitality, and a bit of a focal point at that. In this case it meant "sip" but can't "spit" and worse I had continual refills from our generous hosts. As I was clearly enjoying the refreshments, I was handed Rosie's, Freddie's and Polly's as well. As I was glad we were in a dry warm shelter, I decided to grin and bear it, as I didn't want to upset our hosts.

The rain finally stopped and we returned outside into the village, thanking our hosts through Dobbla. Afterwards he said to me "Sir, I didn't know you liked Yak-butter tea so much; I didn't think it was good so I didn't drink mine".

We started walking, partially dried out. We were

accompanied by a local villager who said we had to watch out for wild dogs. Sure enough, heading down the slope from the village, half a dozen or so normal but clearly undomesticated dogs were following us, barking with excitement, and paying attention to Rosie and Freddie. Having grown up with dogs I recognised the behaviour and pack mentality immediately, so became concerned. Dobbla, our new friend, and I had to throw stones and small rocks to deter them. After a few misses I managed to hit the pack leader with a half-kilo rock from 30-40 yards, an impressive throw. It sent him off yelping and limping and the rest of the pack dissipated. My school years playing cricket were clearly not wasted after all.

We carried on down the slope, drying as we went until we reached the campsite, by a river in the final valley before the walk to Rongbuk the next day.

Descending from the pass, a very soggy family look forward to drying out in air-conditioned tents.

Luckily for us, the route from the village to the campsite was almost entirely downhill, which allowed us to maintain our morale despite being damp. A couple of hours before camp the clouds broke, allowing the sun to shine and for us to dry out somewhat.

EBC TIBET – DAY 4

Zommug to Rongbuk (4980m)

The day started slowly with Rosie and Freddie both feeling the effects of being wet and cold the previous day. If ever there was a day to take a break, this should have been it. After breakfast, which was barely edible (I can't even remember what it was, other than coffee), we set off. Some sweets helped Rosie and Freddie along.

The view from our campsite, at the base of Lamna La Pass, looking towards the Rongbuk and Everest region.

We met some cyclists from the UK enroute who we had seen earlier. I'm not sure which is better, walking or cycling. Using a bike may well be faster, but you would see a lot less. I warned them about the dogs on the way back to Tingri. We carried on up the valley, mostly flat with some gentle inclines along a sandy track. We walked until we saw the first real view of Everest through the valley in the distance, it was quite a sight. We hadn't seen the mountain on the trek before now, only on a day trek the previous week, from perhaps 50 miles away. The day was long and horrible; on approach to Rongbuk the track is shared with traffic, and there was a lot of road construction taking place. We eventually reached Rongbuk after going through a police checkpoint, where we had to show our passports and permits. Rongbuk monastery sits in the first open valley with a fantastic view of Everest. On arrival it was cloudy, so we could not see the mountain clearly but it was a "changeable" day and fortunately before nightfall virtually all the clouds had left. Our campsite was on the grass just downhill from the monastery steps; a great place to sleep for the night.

A happy couple relieved to have Everest finally in sight! The campsite was in the green field just downhill from the monastery.

Freddie was suffering from exhaustion or lack of food, so we made sure both kids had a meal and a good night's sleep. The cook actually managed to provide something edible, simply pasta, so I ate as much as possible. I was personally feeling very tired now after the few days of walking and carrying gear, but was looking forward to our last leg of the trip to EBC the next day.

The cook approached us that night to tell us that his wife was ill and he had to return home. We said our goodbyes, and became concerned that the remaining staff were probably less trained with handling food than he was.

Rosie and Freddie relaxing in their tent prior to the next day's walk to Base Camp.

EBC TIBET – DAY 5

Rongbuk to EBC (5200m)

EBC day started with fabulous views of Mt. Everest; we were feeling tired but motivated to make one last effort to complete the journey. Both Rosie and Freddie were in good spirits, especially with being told that today's walk would be shorter than previous days. It didn't mean much to them because they weren't entirely sure whether to believe it or not.

Monks relaxing by our tents, with the north face of Mt. Everest behind.

Breakfast was inedible again. I think I managed a couple of boiled eggs but Rosie and Freddie refused to eat (as did

Polly). We set off, taking some glorious photos of a sun-drenched skyline.

Starting the walk from Rongbuk to Everest Base Camp - a glorious day!

After a couple of hours we made it to the "tented village", where you can buy some material souvenirs and have some food. We stopped for a break with the kids sharing a noodle dish. Polly commented there that the food was much better than on trek, and there was no reason for the trekking staff not being able to provide cooked food to the same standard.

Rosie and Freddie both required a chocolate bribe to start moving again. There was a strong temptation just to relax and stay there! We carried on walking with Dobbla, who was saying slightly too much "we're almost there, just another half an hour".

Fabulous views along the way from Rongbuk to Base Camp.

He never realised that our kids can tell the time and so kept asking me why the guide couldn't get his timings right. The approach from the tented village to EBC is very rocky and follows a track, which meanders between steep-sided scree slopes of metamorphic and heavily deformed rock. I was left thinking at one point that I wouldn't want to be at the base of the scree if an earthquake hit. As we were meandering through the scree slopes we had lost sight of Everest, and we wouldn't see it again until EBC itself. The lack of view meant that the track seemed to go on forever. At 5000m+ you can clearly feel the strength of the sun on your skin, and the air is so thin it felt like you needed to focus on not exerting too much effort. We were so close. The last thing we'd want was for one of us to feel altitude effects. After a couple of hours we stopped for a break, with our guide promising that we were only 20 minutes away. We couldn't see beyond the scree so didn't know what to believe, although obviously we must have been getting close.

A long walk along dirt tracks towards the Base Camp area.

We set off for what would be our last time and soon joined a paved road with occasional prayer flags above. Within a few minutes we could see the EBC area with Everest beyond.

One last push through freezing winds to Base Camp.

My legs were truly feeling it now. All I could do was just focus on not exerting myself. Rosie joined me to hold my hand. I just thought of how amazing our kids had been, walking 70km plus some, through desert conditions, high and low temperatures, very wet and windy storms, and didn't complain at all. I was impressed that the kids had walked so far, clearly natural trekkers. I thought that maybe they would like to trek to Machu Picchu or Kilimanjaro next year. Then Rosie said, "Daddy, next year can we go to Hawaii, they've got really good beaches there?" I laughed to myself (avoiding breathing too much) while Rosie gabbled on as usual. This girl can do anything, as long as she gets to chat and have a few sweets! I fully expected the Hawaii topic to come up and wondered if it would happen in the way it did, but it's hilarious it actually came out that way! We carried on walking, with me repeating to myself "almost there, almost there…" while Rosie carried on talking about building sandcastles and playing in the sea. We reached the base of EBC where there is a monolith stating the fact, probably in case you weren't aware (or maybe just lost!) We took a few photos but really the best views were from the small hill behind, smothered in prayer flags. We climbed up the steps and were presented with the most amazing view of Mt. Everest. We had done it. Rosie and Freddie had become perhaps the youngest Westerners to have trekked to EBC. Polly had managed to trek it despite her spinal surgery and I had managed it despite losing about a stone in weight from carrying everyone else's junk.

A very hard-earned and well deserved family photo, and what an incredible journey, especially for 6 and 7-year olds!

We stayed a while, taking lots of obligatory photos. One of the guards, a 19-year old Chinese soldier, tried to stop us from using a banner which marked the achievement, but I argued with him that it was for a school photo, so he gave in eventually. We also returned the following day from Rongbuk to crystal clear views and what will probably be our ultimate family holiday snapshot.

Back at Rongbuk we relaxed with tea and biscuits before visiting the monastery. Rosie received a blessing from the head Lama intended to release her from the fear of thunder. Travelling through Tibet can be a very spiritual experience. It is clear why so many people value the true Tibetan culture so highly. We headed back to the border the next day, having to take a helicopter flight to Kathmandu to avoid monsoonal landslides enroute.

On the plane journey back to the UK, Rosie and Freddie again just looked like two normal kids, both sitting down on their seat, with headphones on watching the airline cartoon channel. "How is that possible?" I thought to myself. "There is no way they should have been able to do that" - the kids were just amazing.

A Rongbuk monk looks back towards Everest.

THE NEPAL EARTHQUAKE

On April 25th 2015 the Himalayan region was shaken by a magnitude 8.1 earthquake

In London, the morning of Saturday 25th April 2015 was looking like a fairly normal spring day. It was dry and sunny, and I was enjoying a slow start to it after a busy week at work. My aim was to relax and take it slowly, so I didn't get out of bed until after 8.00 am. My normal commute had tired me out for the weekend. I rolled out of bed, stumbled downstairs and put the kettle on to make some coffee. Rosie and Polly were up already and I heard them close the front door behind them – Rosie was chatting about what they needed from the corner shop. The volume of her voice grew smaller as she walked down the street. On checking the fridge, there was just enough milk for one cup. I put the kettle on, made myself a mug, yawned and walked to the living room. I sat in one corner of the sofa with my drink and looked for the remote control. I switched the TV on and relaxed. A news channel came on. I saw red brick rubble, dust and the familiar voice of a news reporter on the phone urgently reporting a major story. What's this? My brain worked quickly to piece together what the news was. Collapsed buildings. Dust. My heart raced faster – was this a terror attack? Could it be in London? Map of Nepal. "Earthquake". "Kathmandu". People hurt.

Stunned silence in my mind.

As I watched I could feel the blood drain from my face. I could hear my heart beat louder. The horror moved from the subconscious to my conscious mind. We had just been there. Pictures streamed in showing one of the main squares in Kathmandu in ruins. Clearly there would be a lot of casualties.

Rosie's voice started to grow louder as she and Polly returned to the house. I rushed to the front door and opened it for them. I knew Polly would be upset. She had spent a lot of time in the city and used it as a base for trekking, and had also taught there many years earlier.

"There's been an earthquake – in Nepal", I said, trying to control myself.

"What! Is it bad?" Polly asked.

We sat down and watched the news reports come in for some time, both in a state of shock. "Those poor people. You do realise this is my second home, don't you?", Polly said with a tear in her eye. "I love Nepal." We watched as more reports came in throughout the day. It was clear it was a devastating disaster. "You do realise that some towns will be completely destroyed, don't you? They are only reporting from Kathmandu – the other older towns will be badly hit", Polly said.

The effects of the earthquake were felt nearly 200km away at Everest, with an avalanche killing at least 19 people on the Nepalese Everest Base Camp. We wondered what had happened in Tibet. News reports from further afield were few and far between, with the remoteness and difficulty in reporting from Tibet limiting news from across the border. The apparent lack of reporting in the media from China's remotest region highlighted its isolation.

Over the following days the true scale of the disaster became evident. I thought about what we could do. Polly asked if I would look after the kids while she went to Nepal to help. I understood where she was coming from but we weren't in a position to do that. I had a busy job and we had no-one to help with our kids for an extended period of time. Surely there were other things we could do?

CHAPTER THREE – FUTURE PLANS

In the year following our Tibetan trek, we considered where to go next. We somewhat debated Kilimanjaro or Maccu Pichu, although strictly speaking the kids were too young to easily get permits. The kids had done very well in Tibet and had coped well with the high altitude. After the trip we met with a reporter from the Daily Telegraph who took an interest in our Tibetan adventure, especially given the age of Rosie and Freddie at the time. The paper decided not to publicise our trip as framing the story was an issue for them. I was under the impression they liked stories in destinations which fit with a commercial need rather than reporting on the physical achievement of such young kids, or maybe they couldn't verify the story despite our photos. We were slightly disappointed as we felt Rosie and Freddie deserved some recognition. The lack of awareness of those close to us also didn't help – few people recognized what an achievement it was, unless shown photos of the trip. I found this slightly infuriating – people seemed to take more of an interest in a neighbour's day at the beach, as that is what most people can relate to. Polly and I agree that we should be living somewhere with a more adventurous culture!

I proposed to Polly that we do it again, this time in Nepal itself. We felt that we could help promote trekking in Nepal at a time when it was needed. Perhaps this was how we could help after the earthquake. She was naturally cautious initially, as she didn't want to lose holiday time in the summer and doubted whether the trekking companies would accept 7 and 9 year-old children. I promised her that it wouldn't affect our summer trips. She agreed and this time I took the lead in making the arrangements, again using the same Nepalese company, Himalayan Expeditions.

The trek itself would be over very different topography to the Tibetan side, so would raise a new set of challenges. I spent quite some time emailing the trekking company in Kathmandu, trying to ensure that the plan was achievable from Rosie and Freddie's point of view. The company were happy to take us again, having previously worked with us in Tibet. We were later told that their most experienced trek leader, Ricky, would be our guide. Ricky had told the company that what we were planning was simply impossible and could not be done by children of that age. His own contacts within the Nepalese guide community were not familiar with Everest base camp treks being made with kids of that age range. He was sent a dossier of information on us regarding our Tibetan experience to help convince him that it may be feasible, and also to highlight what we thought the issues may be. He used this brilliantly to tailor or trip to ensure we were happy with the trek organisation itself.

On this next trek we would be squeezed for time, with the main trekking season being at Easter, when the kids had a much more limited time off school. The timing worked both for and against us. The Easter holidays were towards the end of March in 2016, so the weather in Nepal would only just be warming up, not fully into Spring. At home, this meant that our practice hillwalking days would still be in the winter. Although not good news on the face of it, it did mean that the kids experienced walking at the snowline, at Snowdon, which actually made sense in preparation for Everest. The cold weather in the UK also allowed us to test the kids outdoor cold weather gear, and it highlight were gaps may have been.

Obviously we hoped we would not have to use extreme weather gear in Nepal. In the run-up to our trip departure I started to monitor mountain-forecast.com, for an indication of the conditions we could expect.

Everest Trekking With Kids

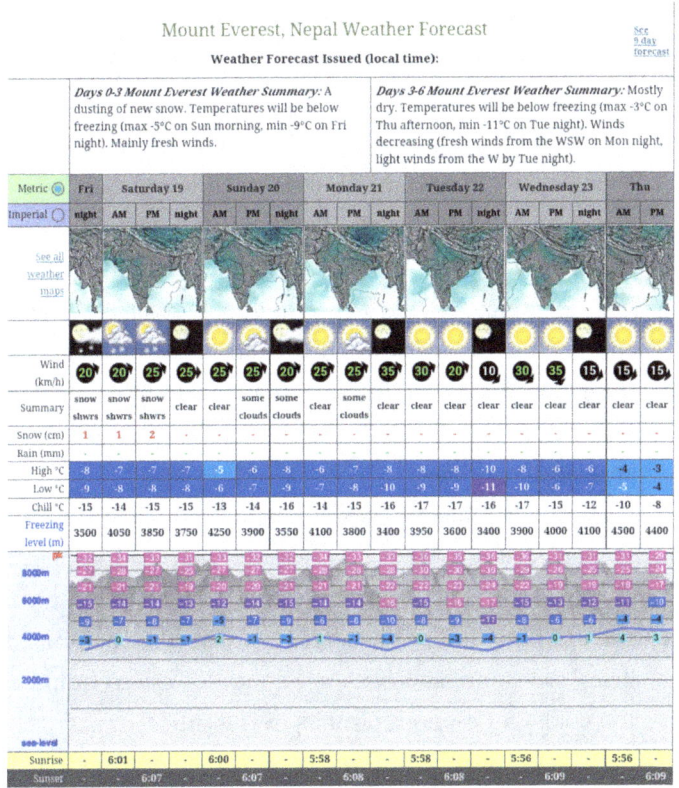

Mountain-forecast.com highlights the expected temperature at various elevations. Here the prediction was always sub-zero with a hint of milder weather on the way from March 23rd, closer to the start of our trek.

The temperatures at Everest between 4000-6000m, most of our trekking altitude window, stayed stubbornly well below freezing as the departure date approached. On March 20th, just a couple of days before departure from the UK, the 4000-6000m temperature prediction was -5 to -9 degrees Celsius, with freezing level at 3550m. If this continued all but the first two days would be well below freezing.

"Could the kids cope with walking and sleeping in this?" I asked myself.

On the bright side I knew from bitter experience that -9 C in the UK, with damp air, feels much worse than the same temperature with dry air. Rosie and Freddie had already experienced -16C a few years earlier on a ski trip to Canada, but they were now much older and more resilient. I checked and double checked with other sources, with the consensus being that during the day it would be cold but perhaps not freezing at lower altitudes, and at night time it would be absolutely perishing.

It was for this reason we bought both kids the warmest synthetic (stays warm even when wet) sleeping bags, rated to -28 degree C, along with the warmest base layers we could find. In hindsight, neither Rosie nor Freddie complained at being too warm, and neither did they lose sleep from being too cold. Our cautious planning was justified.

A day or two before we departed, there were at last hints of more mild weather approaching from 24th March, our first full trekking day having an estimated freezing level at 4400m. I hoped that this would be the sign that Spring was arriving, and our trek would not be curtailed by poor weather.

We departed London, with the expectation of a brilliant and exciting adventure ahead.

CHAPTER FOUR – EVEREST BASE CAMP TREK, NEPAL

Day 1

The start of the trek was scheduled to involve a quick dash from Kathmandu's Dwarika's hotel to the airport followed by a few hours introductory walking to the first overnight stay in Phadking. On arrival at the domestic airport terminal in Kathmandu we made our way to the Goma airlines check-in desk, one of several flying to Lukla that morning. Fairly quickly it became obvious that delays were occurring. Looking around we noted that there were not that many kids around, with Rosie and Freddie being by far the youngest westerners there. Several trekkers on our flight tried to queue-jump, incorrectly assuming that as we had young kids we simply couldn't have been checking in for Lukla. After a few hours of poor weather conditions at Lukla the flight was cancelled. I checked with one of the helicopter tour company's what they would charge for 5 of us (family plus Ricky), around $2000 I recall, and while the cost was not totally unreasonable, it wasn't justifiable for us as we had two or three days flexibility on our trip anyway. We decided to go back to the hotel and try again the following day.

Waiting to check-in at Kathmandu for the short flight to Lukla, frequently called the world's most dangerous airport.

We were successful! The flight took off, slightly delayed, for its 30 minute hop to Lukla. Comfortable enough, our small plane was thrown around over one of the high passes five minutes before landing, with Rosie crying somewhat. This was not the worst turbulence I had experienced but given the context it caused a bit of a stir on board, with a few gasps on every bump, some laughter and fortunately no screaming. On landing, the passengers cheered and applauded, both in relief at landing safely and this marking the start of everyone's adventure over the next few weeks. One of the passengers turned and said to Rosie in sympathy "See…perfectly OK if a bit scary, but we were fine!" I attempted to calm Rosie further by saying "Yeah - you've just got to do it again on the way back!" to some laughter. I didn't seem to help her that much.

We departed the plane and were guided to a teahouse for lunch before the trek started. We watched planes safely arrive and depart from all the local airlines - Goma, Yeti and Tara. Ricky introduced us to Kazi, our second guide and Sherpa for the trip.

Planes taking off from Lukla - the short runway is on a slope running downhill for take-offs, so landing is uphill.

Previously Ricky had spoken to us in Kathmandu, with Polly and I agreeing that he had doubts as to whether the kids would make it to EBC, probably as he had never taken young children to base camp before. I reassured her saying that we needed to give him a chance to see how the kids coped with walking, and also that the agency had indicated to me that the team supplied were very experienced, unusually so in fact for such a small family group. Polly had not been involved with the detailed planning of this particular trip, whereas normally she likes to oversee every detail of the itinerary. Polly and I were struck immediately by the special warmth emanating from Kazi, over the next couple of weeks it became clear that he is one of the most thoughtful and generous people we have ever met. We felt very well looked after by him. Ricky, as group leader, was obviously more in charge of the staff so was more distant, something the kids worked their magic on over the next few days. The remainder of the crew, who we got to know better during the trek, consisted of Syem, who would serve the single best pizza I have ever tasted, cooked using basic utensils on a mountain side, cook's helpers, porters and Yak herder Annie.

Our first day's trek was from Lukla to Phakding. It took 3 hours to reach our first campsite outside a teahouse. As we had packed our backpacks as hand-luggage for the flight, I had found myself trekking with all sorts of electronic gadgetry including a new heavy laptop and some books. My backpack must have weighed 15kg, something I was able to reduce to below 10kg in the following days. The rest of the luggage and camp gear were carried by yaks and porters. When travelling with yaks, one thing to remember which impacted on our ability to be flexible in doing the trek was the amount of food they carried. On one occasion later in the trek, we requested an itinerary change to allow slower adjustment to AMS. Normally this is not allowed or considered, but as we were a private group, with kids as well, the itinerary change was agreed to by Ricky. However, there were not enough rations for the crew or hay for the yaks, so the adjustment involved only the main trekking party (family plus two guides), with the remainder of the group having to go on a diversion to collect rations. Polly and the kids also carried daypacks. Again as the "daddy" of the family, with unimaginable and limitless strength, my bag tended to be heavier than the others. Looking at Ricky though, I had some way to go to compete! My advice for day one of the trek is to be careful what you pack, and when departing the plane find an opportunity to repack if necessary – keep the daypacks light!

The walk itself was straightforward on dirt tracks, a bit of up and down through some villages, all below 3000m, so no altitude concerns. The start of the trek is marked by the Memorial Gate, a green arch supported by two white pillars.

Between here and the National Park entrance there are few culturally interesting localities. Today the skies were overcast and deeply atmospheric, great for photos but perhaps a little concerning for trekkers. We passed large Mani stones with Tibetan prayer wheels alongside. These are dark with white text painted on, and are religious offerings in Tibetan Buddhism. The small villages were made more colourful with brightly painted prayer wheels. Later on this walk we encountered the first of several suspension bridges, which became more impressive in scale further up the valley. All traffic, be it trekkers, locals or yaks use the bridges to cross the valley, which enlarges into a much deeper canyon further uphill. There are no roads from Lukla so all luggage, camping and expedition materials are carried on the trek route by porters or yaks. No matter how heavy you might imagine your backpack to be, the sight of a porter carrying enormous packs puts everyone else to shame. On one day we even saw a porter carry a full-sized fridge on his back towards one of the teahouses enroute.

The campsite at Phakding was good. Our routine would involve the staff cooking our meals using teahouse facilities and we would then eat in the teahouses. At Phakding, the first common stop on the trek, it was clear Rosie and Freddie were the youngest people there by quite some margin.

It is worth pointing out that no other parties were camping at the same time, the next expedition tents we would see would be one day before EBC itself at Gorak Shep. "Were we mad camping given the freezing overnight temperatures?" Polly asked. Ricky said that the advantage of camping was that the expedition team had control of the food preparation, so he knew exactly what we were eating and had complete control over hygiene. We did spend a few nights at higher altitude sleeping in teahouses, as the night-time temperature fell to minus 10 degrees Celsius. Travelling with kids and the morning routine of preparing for the day ahead was certainly faster in teahouses.

The kids at the Memorial Gate, marking the formal start to the Everest Base Camp trek in Nepal.

EBC NEPAL – DAY 2

Phakding to Namche Bazar (3440m)

The next day we headed north towards Namche Bazar at 3440m. Group after group of trekkers and yak herds, carrying expedition supplies, passed us and vice versa. As we headed on, the weather became warmer and drier.

Mani stones enroute from Lukla

We passed a few villages with more large Mani stones. As we headed up the valley we started to gain altitude. We crossed a few of the amazing bridges over the canyon, which became deeper as we gained altitude. Polly and Rosie were very wary of the height of the bridges and the drop to the river below, but crossed with a good sense of humour.

Our guide Kazi

The suspension bridges are made from strong steel cables and a metal walkway, and are very well maintained. The sides, from the cable handhold to feet, are protected with wire mesh, making falling off the side virtually impossible. The metal construction easily supports the weight of the many yak herds which make their way up and down the valley. Vibrant colour is added by the many prayer flags tied to the sides, which also act as good wind strength indicators! Although the bridges can be very high, they seem very strong and of no concern from a safety point of view.

At one of the bridges, we met with Jelle Veyt, a Flemish mountaineer who had cycled from Belgium to make his third summit attempt. He was very friendly and loved the sight of the kids, asking if he could video them on the bridge for Dutch national television. Obviously we agreed although Rosie didn't want to spend time on the bridge so only Freddie went. We met Jelle quite a few times over the next few days as we would leapfrog each other's progress – he had a lot of time to acclimatise before his May summit attempt so he was taking it slowly. We carried on, reaching Namche Bazar late in the day after an arduous climb. The weather was fairly mixed with a lot of cloud, and the walk very tiring, I don't think I took many photos as we spent a lot of time making sure we weren't suffering from altitude effects. It was also very cold as we approached Namche Bazar, and we felt like we wouldn't like to camp.

One of the fantastic suspension bridges enroute. The Tibetan prayer flags are a useful wind speed indicator - but the bridges are very safe.

Namche Bazar is a market town on the steep flanks of the valley. Walking from the lower parts of the village to the top where our teahouse was situated was an effort. The village was affected by the earthquake, with the main stupa at the village entrance being heavily cracked, with the supporting base now shattered but still in place. We concluded that heavy monsoonal rains later in the year might cause further damage. It was such a shame that such a picturesque village had been scarred in this way, but at least the physical damage did look repairable. As we would later observe in Kathmandu and Bhaktapur, the Everest trek region seemed to be affected less than elsewhere in Nepal, probably due to the lower population density and lower levels of development. In Namche Bazar, all of the buildings still looked intact from the outside.

Arrival at Namche Bazar, a very colourful village at the start of the higher altitude zone.

Namche Bazar is within the high altitude zone, and we could feel the effects with slightly sore heads when we arrived. We stayed in a pre-booked "luxury lodge", although this was one or two stars by western standards. It had a restaurant, flushing loos and - wait for it - electric blankets! When we entered the room we liked the appearance. Polly had sussed the electric blankets quite quickly, Freddie came inside, put his hands under one of the double beds, felt the heat and jumped into the air screaming "Yes! Wahoo!" which was hilarious, as if we had won the lottery! We had been cold for some time!

The main stupa in Namche Bazar was badly damaged by the 2015 earthquake.

On the walk to Namche, the last couple of hours were the hardest, with effects of the thinner air being felt. Sleeping that night, although very comfortable, the thinner air meant we had to stay hydrated. My resting heart-rate was in excess of 100 beats per minute in the middle of the night, whereas normally it is around 60 – clearly the signs of my body re-adjusting to the new environment.

EBC NEPAL – DAY 3

Namche Bazar, acclimatisation day.

We woke up, Polly and the kids were fine but I had a sore head all night and didn't feel great. Breakfast helped slightly. The aim of today was simply to go to the Everest Hotel at 3880m, where normally there are good views.

Acclimatisation walk above Namche Bazar.

Today though was overcast and foggy. We had all day for the short climb so we moved very slowly. The kids asked for quite a lot of breaks on the walk, so I said we'd measure every

50m attitude climb and then stop for a drink. Having an altimeter on my watch would prove to be very useful in monitoring our progress. The pace seemed about right for our kids, although Rosie also started to get a sore head on the way up. Ricky said that by going up to the hotel and back down again, the action would acclimatise us to the altitude of Namche, now beneath us, and help with the following day. Half-way to the hotel we stopped so the kids could play noughts and crosses with their trekking poles in the soil, something they enjoyed so we let them play to help slow the pace and also to make sure they were having some fun!

The trail is shared with plenty of yak trains and other trekkers.

It was cold, overcast with no real view so not the most enjoyable of conditions to walk in, so moments of fun were very welcome. At the hotel we all had tomato soup to take on some liquids, which also helped with the cold. On the way down, we all felt much better and by that afternoon were fine, so walked around Namche looking around the shops at the local wares. Polly had spotted some yak bells on sale and as usual managed to barter for a better deal. The kids bought some Everest key rings for their school bags back home.

The weather in Namche was dull and overcast, as we were basically within the cloud layer.

Rosie and Freddie with our two guides, Ricky and Kazi.

EBC NEPAL – DAY 4

Namche Bazar to Deboche (3820m)

Today's plan was to walk to Phungi Thanga for lunch and then onto Deboche at 3820m, visiting Tengboche Monastery enroute.

The day was overcast and it started to rain as we walked. Enroute to Deboche, Ricky mentioned to Polly that we would pass Khumjung, where there is 'Yeti scalp' kept in a local museum. Before we had travelled to Nepal, we suggested to the kids that there might be the chance of spotting a Yeti in this part of the Himalayas, and they would have to keep an eye out while trekking. Polly asked Ricky if we could make a diversion to visit the museum at Khumjung. When we arrived the museum was locked. Ricky tried to find someone with the key but we eventually ran out of time and had to move on. The kids kept themselves entertained, playing with a large prayer wheel next door and making friends with the local dogs.

The Sherpa community actually distinguish three types of Yeti, but we had failed to find anyone who had claimed to have seen one. The scalp had previously been borrowed by Edmund Hillary and taken to North America and Europe for scientific tests. Reports suggested that the Yeti scalp was more of a ceremonial hat but over time had gained the status of being a real scalp. Nevertheless, our enduring search for a Yeti on trek helped keep the kids' minds focussed, as part of our overall strategy to keep the trip as fun as possible for them. Khumjung also sports the Edmund Hillary School as well as a statue of the great man. It was very misty, wet and quite cold at this point on our trip. We decided to continue our trek towards Phungi Thanga.

Ricky mentioned that today, March 31st, was a special day, and the kids eventually guessed that it was his birthday. I told him that he was lucky not to be born on April 1st. On trek, we observed some of the Nepalese wildlife, including the Danfe, the very colourful National bird and some rare mountain goats. At Tengboche, we spotted a bakery! Given the circumstances and the special day, Polly and I decided to treat the kids and Ricky with a large slice of homemade chocolate cake from us. Despite being far from his family and friends we wanted Ricky to feel part of our family and have a birthday cake to celebrate. Given that we were also gaining altitude and moving into ever more remote areas, I was also concerned that the chocoholics in our group (i.e. everyone) might become grouchy if we missed the opportunity!

The trekking path is maintained by a small team of locals, who rely on donations. Freddie signs a visitor book.

At Deboche, it became overcast again, which kept us cool if not a little bit on the cold side. I hoped the weather would improve, as we wanted better views on this trip! At the teahouse campsite, we were in bed by 9pm. A few people in the teahouse thought it was better to be inside than camp outside in the cold, but in the morning they complained at the teahouse rooms only being 6 degrees overnight, whereas the tents were a similar 5 degrees although felt warmer. It is clearly harder to heat a whole room with body heat than a two-person tent! Sharing body heat meant it didn't quite feel as cold as it could have done. Later on the trek we would realise that 5 or 6 degrees was pure luxury!

EBC NEPAL – DAY 5

Deboche to Dingboche (4410m)

This morning we had glorious views of Everest, although the views became obscured throughout the day as we moved along. Our heads were all clear, Rosie and Freddie enjoyed the long walk. We were definitely gaining altitude, leaving the treeline well behind.

The trek is a mostly a very visual experience for obvious reasons. The sense of sound is also engaged by a few things in particular. Firstly, what makes this trek different to others is the sound of the prayer flags flapping in the wind, where otherwise there would be absolute silence, which in itself is also remarkable to experience. The second feature fairly unique to Nepal, is the reassuringly slow tones ringing from the yak bells. Although not a unique sound in itself, the pattern of having the bells approach from a distance and pass safely encourages trekkers to stop, which in turn gives them more time to experience the trekking environment.

Our campsite outside the teahouse at Debouche, covered in frost. This was our first morning with clear skies giving fabulous views of the surrounding peaks, which had been obscured by cloud the previous day.

As we walked along the base of the valley, we become surrounded by more high peaks. In the distance the most spectacular was Ama Dablam, often described as Nepal's most beautiful mountain. At 6812m tall and being very visually impressive it is often the subject of many climbing expeditions, and also makes a great backdrop to photos and artwork in Nepal. Carrying on, we gained altitude gradually, walking along a path to one side of the valley, crossing more suspension bridges. Before turning into the valley where Dingboche sits, there was one last steep climb up the flanks of the valley. Despite looking like it would take forever, with the kids being quite slow at this point, we climbed maybe 200m in less than two hours including several stops. As we turned north towards Dingboche the slope became much more gentle, and we started looking forward to reaching our destination for the day.

Ama Dablam is one of the most beautiful peaks in the Everest trekking area. At 6812m it is often the objective of climbing expeditions.

Dingboche sits in a relatively flat area of a wide valley, presumably where two alluvial fans coalesce, making the ground more suitable for farming as well as building on. It is surrounded by spectacular peaks and slopes leading even higher to the north towards Mt. Everest, which was now hidden from view. Dingboche village is made up of a couple of hundred grey brick buildings with very distinctive green and blue rooftops. Walking through the village it clearly functions as both a farming base and also to support trekking and climbing groups. Other than the teahouses there was little commercial activity except for a basic bakery and café.

After dumping our bags at the teahouse, where we would be for two nights, we set out to explore a little. Ricky asked us not to walk uphill or downhill so he could track how we were acclimatising. Luckily the café was within a short walk from the teahouse, where the kids had a cake treat and we had some decent coffee. It was now very cold and foggy, with us being in the middle of the cloud layer. We hoped that as we went higher we would leave the cold and wet conditions behind and have better views again.

Back at the teahouse the camping staff made us dinner, serving it in the communal area with everyone else, perhaps 40 other people. Again it was clear - there were no other children trekking. The cold weather and new altitude had triggered the Khumbu cough amongst many, including myself. At one point the coughing became psychologically contagious, with each person triggering someone else in the room, until virtually the entire teahouse was coughing en mass, gradually reaching a crescendo, followed afterwards by fits of laughter.

Having kids made us the centre of attention, or so it seemed. No doubt many people were wondering if we were headed to base camp, and would have been thinking whether that was possible or not. We broke the ice with a few of the trekkers with photos of Rosie and Freddie at base camp in Tibet.

At Dingboche the clouds and fog set in, and again the night was very cold. We stayed at a local teahouse. The atmosphere was very friendly and jovial with a natural surprise initially at seeing young kids on the trek.

Later while Polly and the kids had gone for a walk, one local talked about the earthquake with a couple of trekkers, huddled around the central fire for warmth, and how he had seen people die in the avalanche. He spoke gently but loud enough to be heard by everyone in the teahouse. Otherwise there was silence as people listened and pretended to continue reading their books or playing card games. He talked about it continually, having the effect of dampening the spirits in the teahouse with the atmosphere becoming more serious. I felt sorry for him. This was a tricky situation, obviously trekkers know the risks and sympathise but were also there to have an enjoyable trip, and were helping those affected just by being in Nepal. I put the man's demeanour down to psychological damage from the shock of seeing what had happened and wondered how he was going to move on from those tragic events.

Approaching Dingboche with Ama Dablam as a backdrop.

EBC NEPAL – DAY 6

Dingboche, Acclimatisation Day.

Finally the skies looked like they were clearing! In reality we later discovered the clouds had just moved downhill, so we were now above the cloud-line. We set off on our acclimatisation walk above Dingboche.

Preparing to leave Dingboche in the morning for the start of the day's acclimatisation.

Leaving the village, the kids asked very enthusiastically, "What is the man in the field doing?" On looking, he was using a yak to tow an old plough, for the planting of potatoes. He had just start ploughing the field so had only a few lengths of soil overturned. This reminded me of a similar scene in Cambodia many years earlier, where a water-buffalo was being used. The question highlights the huge difference in culture between Nepal and the modern world. In this location, with no road transport either, the locals would have been forced into using local resources rather than importing a tractor – the only way that would have been possible would be to fly one in by helicopter, or carried piece by piece and then reconstructed, and then there would be also be a fuel supply issue to deal with as well. Here, half way up a large mountain range, the only access route was by the narrow track we had walked on from the National Park entrance. This was new for Rosie and Freddie, they had never seen animals being used in this way for farming. I was pleased that they were taking a keen interest, as it showed their minds were alert and physically fit, and they were not suffering from AMS.

Taking it slowly, we have great views of the village below.

As we walked further up the track, local women, dressed in traditional costume, were spending their time sorting potatoes, laying them out in the sun. The kids were transfixed by this, whereas Ricky and Kazi were oblivious as to why this might be an interesting scene for westerners. As we walked past, the scene was like stepping back in time, with the locals being completely at ease with us. In Tibet by comparison, it was much more difficult to get close to the locals, we felt much more controlled in what we could or could not see, so our interactions were more limited.

Tibetan prayer flags add colour to the amazing views.

Acclimatisation walk above Dingboche, with a view of the spectacular scenery to come.

Again as we climbed above Dingboche we stopped frequently, using a stupa as a natural resting point for food and water. Stones had been gathered in stacks around the stupa, and then lines of prayer flags connected the rocks to the central point in radial patterns. Having the white stupa in the foreground, framed with the many colourful prayer flags blowing in the wind, and with incredible snow-capped peaks in the background completed a truly memorable and stunning view.

Looking back towards Dingboche, the clouds had clearly retreated to a lower altitude further down the valley. We were now higher than the clouds, and it would remain that way for most of the remaining trip towards base camp.

Many groups were on the acclimatisation climb today, with a huge slope on the hillside above the village allowing plenty of scope for an acclimatisation walk to suit everyone's taste. Ricky said that we would climb 300m, although if he had other stronger adult groups then he sometimes went further. Indeed some groups looked like they were going much higher. We thought that people should be sensible about it, perhaps not pushing themselves too hard in case they trigger an illness or just knacker themselves. We went slowly with the kids, again in the higher parts of our climb we stopped at least every 50m if not more frequently, with the kids enjoying Ricky and Kazi's company. The views were simply spectacular, and this was the first real day when I started focussing on videoing our trip in more detail. The weather helped as well so both Polly and I were enjoying the amazing views. After Ricky got to his 300m altitude increase (my own watch measured it at a bit less at around 250m) we stopped for some lunch, and used the time to admire the scenery. We watched several groups descend from a lot higher, and wondered if they were being too adventurous. They certainly looked well so we could only assume they were all fine. We descended after lunch and headed back to the teahouse where we were staying. Polly made friends with a Lebanese female trekker, who was part of a group of eight individuals. She was clearly unwell, suffering with a bad cold and altitude issues. Polly generously offered medication, as her group seemed less well prepared, and they started talking. Rosie joined them and they went for a walk, maybe window shopping together I thought, although I very much doubted whether Dolce & Gabbana had opened a local Dingboche store – but they did find another coffee shop apparently which was more Polly's style! This was about as good as it got around here! While they were away, I played chess and draughts with Freddie, who was later challenged by Kazi. Freddie managed to outwit him, which I was impressed by. Later Ricky would join in as well.

Ricky enjoys a break with the kids.

Taking kids on this trek route was clearly unusual, we only saw one 12-year-old Indian boy and some teenagers from the UK. When playing draughts with Ricky, a masked Nepalese guy appeared in the teahouse, approached and said to me loudly "Hey - why do you bring kids to the mountains – don't you know it's dangerous here?" I didn't know if he was being deliberately aggressive or just being very direct. I just looked directly at him, didn't flinch, and Ricky quickly waved his arm at him and said "don't listen to him, he's nuts". Later he explained that the local was the same person he talked about a few days earlier, and later I realised was the guy from the previous night. Ricky explained that he was a Nepalese climber with a dream of climbing Everest. He had sold his house, left his job to make the ascent. Then in 2015 when he was hit by the avalanche and saw some climbers killed while on the mountain. Since then he was stuck in limbo with no house, family or job, and was well known by the locals for being badly affected by the quake. It all made sense, and both Polly and I felt sorry for him and hoped he would come to terms with this soon. There must be many people like him throughout Nepal – he was a visible manifestation of the damage that can be done through suffering a major loss in life. We both thought we should make sure we do what we can to help those Nepalese people affected and asked ourselves if we could do more.

EBC NEPAL – DAY 7

Dingboche to Lobuche (4940m)

Today began as another brilliant sunny day with mostly blue skies and a light breeze. We headed off once more, initially following the same route as the previous day's acclimatisation walk. We passed the stupa from the previous day and continued north, up a long wide valley towards Thokla.

Departing Dingboche towards our next stop at Lobuche. Luckily the weather was fantastic giving the most amazing views of the valley and surrounding peaks. The walk is extremely long up a gentle slope before becoming more challenging towards Thokla.

A porter and yak train carry equipment to the higher villages.

The grassy highlands were very open with amazing views of peaks to our left as we walked. The kids enjoyed it, and we met lots of different trek groups heading towards base camp. The walk was slow, at Rosie and Freddie's pace but we still made good progress.

The view looking back towards Dingboche, like others, is eye-watering in its beauty.

A geologist's dream! Great examples of alluvial fan systems and river floodplains coming down the slopes.

Rosie and Freddie enjoy the trekking commentary - "I am knackered" wasn't a common sight but equally as relevant.

Looking towards Thokla, and the steeper slope up to the Everest Memorials.

At Thokla we could see the afternoon's climb, a steep looking 200m climb towards the Everest Memorials, where the likes of Scott Fischer and Tenzing have memorial stacks in their honour. At Thokla we stopped in the teahouse for lunch, with me having a bit of a sore head, with lots of other trekkers looking on at the kids with interest. Syem made one of his most memorable dishes here which included amongst the best onion bajis we had ever tasted. The kids and Polly made a big deal of it, and one of the nearby American groups thought it was hilarious, but agreed they were very good. Later they'd refer to us as "the onion baji family" amongst themselves. After lunch we walked to the memorials, again

On the steep slope above Thokla, we look back to take in the views.

on this steepish uphill we stopped every 30-50m altitude gain. We were overtaken by other groups but we were more concerned about getting there healthily rather than at pace.

The memorials are situated on a wide flat area, with lots of stone stacks representing individuals who have perished whilst on Everest. Most are relatively unknown, but small plaques describe the person represented. Some were climbers who had climbed only once, some had climbed several times and others many. Polly thought the area had a dark and eerie feeling, as it was emotionally intense and thought provoking. We stopped to pay our respects and have a break for the kids before moving on. The rest of the afternoon's walk was a slow gentle uphill to Lobuche with low cloud cover coming in, making it a long day's trek. However, it had been perhaps the most photogenic day we had experienced in many years, with Polly in her element.

At Lobuche we slept in a teahouse as our tent would have been precariously placed on an elevated grassy area with a steep drop, and a newly built hotel to the side restricting access, so hazardous for kids at night-time.

View looking back over the Everest Memorials

One iconic view, looking back towards Dingboche, where we had started the days walk, with Tibetan prayer flags over the Everest memorials.

EBC NEPAL – DAY 8

Lobuche-Gorak Shep (5164m)

The plan was very optimistic today, to climb 230m from Lobuche to Gorak Shep in the morning, rest for a couple of hours, then climb another 200m or so to base camp, dropping back to Lobuche before altitude effects became evident. This was planned as a 10-hour plus day. Myself and

The walk from Lobuche is on a very long rocky path, with many boulders to climb over before reaching Gorak Shep.

Views towards Gorak Shep. In the distance immediately in front is the Khumbu Icefall and EBC.

Polly did not see this happening with the pace we were used to at altitude. We started off from the teahouse at Lobuche with Freddie feeling tired. Progress uphill was slow, with the path being clear and the route being clear. There were several parts of the walk which were very bouldery, particularly towards the end when we walked on the remains of glacial debris.

The altitude increase was starting to catch up on us, with three of us feeling some effects and tiredness. This portion of the walk was very tiring but the views of the surrounding

Walking across boulders en route to Gorak Shep.

mountains were amazing. We focussed on drinking water and slowing the pace, which was at odds with the planned itinerary. Freddie went to the front of our group with Ricky. Polly and I had concerns that he would go too fast, as he likes to be competitive. Given Freddie's natural liking of Ricky, who he was now seeing as a good friend, Freddie wanted to be with him. This was fine by us, but our concern was controlling the pace, so we asked to go slower. We carried on towards Gorak Shep, and there were a lot of other trekkers doing the same with us – the path narrows quite a lot in places so one or two bottle-necks developed. We were shocked at the pace some were going at, and realised that a lot of them must have been taking Diamox. At the teahouse at Lobuche most of the people we spoke to were also on Diamox. Some were feeling altitude effects despite being on it. I thought it was concerning that people would take the drug in the hope that it would help alleviate the symptoms rather than deal with the altitude by controlling pace and fluid intake, but I guess their attitude was influenced by the limited flexibility they had in their schedules, and also that they wanted to be successful! Polly and I had previous high altitude experience so we thought that we shouldn't have had to rely on it. We also decided beforehand that we needed to empathise with and fully understand what Rosie and Freddie were experiencing, so to take medication for our own personal benefit would be unfair on them.

We walked around the final few meanders of the path, now barely visible due to the random spread of boulders, with Gorak Shep now becoming visible. In the distance we could see the first yellow tents of base camp in the far distance. Deceptively base camp looked to be at the same altitude as us, Ricky assured me that it was an optical illusion with it actually being quite a bit higher. We carried on over the path with lots of large boulders. Rosie and Freddie coped well using two walking poles each. I was impressed that they didn't trip or complain about the rocks. The time spent on Snowdon paid off in that regard. The boulder field seemed to be endless, but we persisted until we saw the few buildings which make up Gorak Shep, along with the many trekkers who lined the route. Descending into the village we felt like we could do with a break.

At Gorak Shep, Ricky shows the way!

We rested in the restaurant, having a meal and giving our sore heads time to recover. The plan was to recuperate somewhat before heading off to EBC. We struggled to eat properly with Polly and Freddie in particular starting to feel the effects of altitude more. We paused to monitor our condition, and after a couple of hours it became clear that if anything the altitude effects would become worse not better, which would threaten our chances of making it all the way to base camp. As a precaution Ricky decided that we had to stop our attempt to go to EBC and go downhill, as we did not want to risk Freddie in particular becoming ill with AMS later in the day, which would in turn mean descending after sunset on a dangerous path. Given Freddie's increasing reaction to altitude we positively agreed. We had previously discussed AMS symptoms as a risk to our trip so we accepted the course of action.

That was it we thought - game over. We would not succeed in reaching Everest Base Camp. Despite all of the careful planning and attention paid to altitude acclimatisation we would fail to reach our objective, and being so close made our decision even more galling. Somehow however our journey didn't seem over. Polly and I both said at that point that we still felt destined to be successful so could not understand why this had happened. Rosie started becoming upset and cried a little, saying it wasn't fair that she would miss base camp when she was ok. I told her that we had agreed *we would only do it as a family* and if one of us was ill the rest would have to descend at the same time. I thought we had been so fortunate to be here and was happy that we had done all that we could, so perhaps we would have to accept it wasn't going to be our year, and the trip was still worthwhile. I spoke with a few trekkers as they headed towards base camp and wished that we could be heading in the same direction. We allowed Ricky and Kazi to take Freddie downhill ahead of us to encourage a faster recovery. I said to Ricky as he was leaving that Freddie would recover very quickly, within 100m or so. He headed off while we repacked our bags prior to following on.

We followed behind, with Polly and I discussing why we were feeling the altitude effects more on this day compared to others. We both felt the aim of the day was too optimistic for us, that it should have been a more measured approach from Lobuche – maybe it would have been better for us to acclimatise there for a day, with one following trek day simply going to Gorak Shep, and then doing EBC the next.

We carried on descending to Lobuche disappointed that the trek was over, wondering what we could do and obviously hoping Freddie was feeling better. We still had flexibility in that we did not need to fly from Lukla on day 12 of our trek as originally planned. We knew Freddie would be ok and wondered what games he would be playing on Kazi's smartphone.

As we approached Lobuche we met Ricky, who had started to walk back uphill to meet us. He told us Freddie was settled playing games on Kazi's phone as we had predicted, and told us that he recovered very quickly and was absolutely 100 percent fine, so from his point of view there could be another chance to trek to EBC if we liked, as long as Freddie was feeling fit. We became more upbeat and looking forward to seeing Freddie, and crossed our fingers that tomorrow would bring better luck.

Back at the teahouse Ricky said the following day would be very long, as he was thinking of going from Lobuche to EBC and back, returning further downhill still further to limit the trip delay to a maximum of one more day. This would only be the case if Freddie was still 100 percent in the morning. I called him outside, and told him that I wanted to go slower, taking just one day to go to Gorak Shep, which would be an incredibly slow pace, staying overnight to allow us all to acclimatise as best we could. Then I said we should take the following day to trek to EBC, return to Gorak Shep and then Lobuche. This was the pace that would be best for the kids. He looked somewhat surprised at the request, but as this was a private trip I felt I was entitled to make the demand – he could only say no after all. I had previous discussions with the trekking company around the possibility of adding flexibility onto the trip if altitude was a concern so from my point of view this was a fair request. I was aware that the trip was already delayed and the staff were going to already miss out on free time with their families back home, although they would be paid more. We kept our fingers crossed that Ricky would agree after discussing with his crew.

Ricky came back to us looking happy with a positive smile, saying that they could do it but if there were any more altitude concerns then they would cancel. We agreed and were overjoyed that we might have just one more chance. Ricky said the entire crew had discussed it and wanted us to know that they were right behind us, and they wanted to see the kids being successful. Those comments meant a lot to us.

EBC NEPAL – DAY 9

Lobuche-Gorak Shep

Our second attempt to head towards base camp from Lobuche started very slowly. Given that we had all day for a relatively short walk, Polly and I deliberately waited until late morning to give Freddie extra time to acclimatise, with Polly having already recovered from her sore head at Gorak Shep before the descent. Today was purposely very slow, we wanted to do everything we could to be successful, as we knew we had only one chance remaining. Kazi, Ricky and all four of our family were very well aligned - we'd all go extremely slowly. On the steeper sections of the walk Kazi took the lead to set the pace, with Polly and I occasionally asking him to go even slower. Freddie and Rosie were determined to make it, with Freddie taking every advantage to stop for a break, even when not tired. I was stunned by his determination and adoption of a purposely slow and steady pace.

He started to ask if I could carry his water. I said yes, and then as Polly lifted his rucksack we realised that it was very heavy. On looking inside, Freddie had started his own rock collection, with one sample of each rock type carefully selected. I removed the rocks and water and placed them in my own backpack. He had been carrying a couple of kilos of rock samples! As a geologist myself, it is easy for me to talk about rocks with our kids, with the effect of generating an interest within them. I should have known better myself, the last time we walked before Nepal was around Catbells, when he insisted on carrying a several kilo rock sample, a quartz-rich gneiss, several kilometres back to our car.

As we continued, I monitored his progress on my altimeter, without telling him he was asking for a break with every 25m altitude gain. The walking pace must have looked tediously slow, with Kazi taking as few as 10 steps per minute on the steeper parts of the walk. As we retraced our route from the previous day, we couldn't help feeling that those events actually did us a massive favour with myself certainly feeling much fitter and coping with the thinner air much better. Even Ricky said it looked like the previous day was turning out to be a very good acclimatisation day, if unplanned.

The kids were doing remarkably well. Another British family, with two much older teenagers, had given up at this point with the walk seemingly being too much of a challenge. I wondered if it was due to strong teenage attitudes or perhaps the altitude had zapped their motivation.

We eventually reached Gorak Shep after 4 hours, only an hour slower than the previous day's pace which had caused so many issues. As we had stopped numerous times today we all felt very well hydrated with no sore heads by the time we reached the teahouse. Sleeping in the teahouse, we felt confident and excited that we would reach our objective the following day.

EBC NEPAL - DAY 10

Gorak Shep to EBC (5364m)

Ricky had said that we wanted to avoid further delays and so asked that we start our trek today at 6 a.m., with the plan being to go to EBC, go to the advanced base camp area if we were ok and had time, head back to Gorak Shep and then downwards from there. If we were lucky and fast enough we could get to Periche by nightfall. Polly and I thought that reaching Lobuche was a more likely outcome for the day.

A 6 a.m. start for the walk to EBC - you can feel the cold in the photos!

We set off as planned, feeling massively excited and hopeful that this second attempt would be worth it. The air temperature at 6 a.m. was below minus 10 degrees C, this being well before the time the sun rose above the surrounding peaks.

We were concerned the effect of the cold would have on the kids, so made sure we took both primaloft and down jackets, as well as extra warm gloves and hats in addition to their normal trekking gear. The ground at Gorak Shep had completely frozen overnight, but the skies were clear and it looked like it was going to be a glorious day for us. We carried on, with the path from Gorak Shep towards EBC being increasingly covered with large boulders from glacial deposits. After an hour or so the kids started to complain about the cold, which wasn't that surprising given the temperature. We asked them to wear both their primaloft and down jackets until the sun rose above the mountains.

In the EBC area the sun takes quite some time to rise over the peaks, meaning the temperature is much colder than in Gorak Shep.

Another hour or so and we had base camp well within our sights, with the yellow tents looking like specks against the mammoth rocks and the mountains towering above. The sheer scale of the moraines was impressive.

We observed several small avalanches coming off the peaks, reminding us about the dangers in the area.

Ricky and Kazi point out the peaks and layout of the spectacular Everest amphitheatre. The yellow tents, as specks in the distance mark Base Camp.

Mt. Everest is largely hidden from view in Nepal when in close proximity to base camp, here it can be seen behind Nuptse with the wind creating a peaceful aura around the peak.

A great view of EBC and the Khumbu Icefall to the right.

We carried on taking more photos and videos. As we had set off so early we had the area more or less completely to ourselves. EBC at this time of year was spread over quite a large area, with the prayer flags being at the start of the tented area, where most people stop for the obligatory group photograph. It was our turn to do this. As we approached I simply could not believe what we were about to achieve in the next few moments. The towering peaks around us and the vast ice-sheets were in stark contrast to the two young kids about to reach base camp. The final trek portion leading to EBC is contained within a spectacular amphitheatre of surrounding peaks, creating an amazing sun and wind trap. There was absolute silence, with views of Everest above towering above surrounding peaks. Everest itself had a bright white halo effect around it, created by winds waving around the high summit. We had never seen anything like it before, and felt so lucky to be there in such perfect conditions. We had seen so many young fit looking adults being forced to turn back with altitude-related problems, and we had so nearly had to do this ourselves. As we approached I asked Ricky to go ahead with my camcorder and I asked Polly for us to walk together as a family and reach the prayer flags together. I knew we'd want this on video. Ricky went ahead and filmed us arriving. I was welling up with pride in my kids and in my family at what we had achieved – our kids had become the youngest in the western world to have trekked to Everest base camp, in both Nepal and Tibet. Freddie had already one world record claim in Tibet two years earlier, now we had done something we could be even more proud off. We were the world's first family to have done both base camps. Wow! We reached the prayer flags, with Polly talking for the video record "We did it!" I gave her a huge hug as the tears started. I felt like I was the luckiest dad on the planet, with the most amazing family, I simply could not believe what we had done. I hugged Polly for some time more, thinking about how we had come so very close to not feeling this way! The achievement could so easily have been missed.

We gathered our thoughts as Ricky carried on filming, Rosie was being very energetic with Freddie taking a moment's break. "Wow"- still can't believe what we had done- mind-blowing! I was amazed that all the detailed planning, myself and Polly's previous experience in Tibet, the problems we had en route, we had dealt with it all and we had done it!

"Daddy – can we go to advanced base camp now?" Freddie asked, clearly not that impressed by the small pile of rocks with prayer flags on top, which marked "Everest Base Camp" for most trekkers! The tents in the far distance looked more interesting! We calmed down and told the kids we'd take some photos first. We had planned one in particular for our living room if we made it. In Tibet we designed a banner, Polly's idea, showing some fun Yetis and Everest Base Camp text, to make a good feature for the photo. Back in 2014 I had thought about the design of our Tibetan banner, and considered adding some national flags. We had decided that it was not a good idea in Tibet, as it may have been seen as a political statement – so we kept that one clean. In Nepal however, we had no such issue. We wanted to show our support for the Nepalese people after their earthquake disaster a year earlier. We also knew this would end up in the press, so this time I added the Union Flag and Nepalese national flag, partly due to national pride but mainly to encourage the idea that there are people around the world who do actually care about what happened here. As in Tibet, our guide took lots of photos of us, trying to get the perfect shot. Rosie and Freddie can be difficult when being photographed, with Freddie in particular making silly faces when the chance arises!

On arrival at EBC the kids add to the prayer flags with some of our own bought in Lukla.

We had a quick break to allow the kids some time to tie prayer flags we had brought with us, and then carried on to "advanced base camp". This was basically an uphill extension of EBC with our ultimate destination being the Himalayan Expedition tent area at the foot of the Khumbu icefall, an hour or so extra walking time.

Our ultimate family holiday photo, surpassing our Tibetan version. The photo was used by the Nepali Times in an article publicising our trip to the public when we returned to Kathmandu.

We met with Ricky's friend, a Sherpa, who was preparing the route for the group expedition climbers who would be attempting the summit later in the season. He invited us into the main expedition tent. We drank hot chocolate and talked about the group's summit preparations, the moving icefield and how that was addressed when fixing ladders, as well as the impact of the 2014 avalanche which killed so many Sherpas, and of course the 2015 earthquake.

Walking toward the 'Advanced' area of EBC, an hour or so beyond the prayer flags.

At the Himalayan Expedition climbing tents, at the foot of the Khumbu Icefall.

From the advanced area, looking up at the Khumbu Icefall, which is the start of the Everest summit route.

Normally base camp trekkers are not permitted to mix with expedition teams at base camp, so we were grateful for

Ricky to arrange a meeting so the kids could spend some time inside an expedition tent and meet some climbers. No doubt Rosie and Freddie will be inspired in the future to continue with mountaineering, they were now seeing trekking and climbing as a normal activity. They had now met several expedition groups and had talked to half a dozen or so climbers who would be attempting the summit later in May. Standing at the foot of the Khumbu icefall and looking up at the summit route, seeing only as far as the top of the icefall, I actually thought "Yeah – I could do that". Looking around and up again, the lack of human scale for reference in front of the icefall meant the true scale wasn't fully coming across. Rosie and Freddie have both said since that when they are older they would like to climb Everest – "not until you are at least 18!" Polly would reply.

We said our goodbyes to the expedition team as our time

Polly takes full advantage of the many photo opportunities on the way to EBC.

was running out. The kids spent some time sitting down at the edge of the icefall looking back down towards the start of EBC, with more yak trains arriving with supplies. Ricky was feeling anxious about the schedule. Polly and I were distracted by the amazing experience of having the kids see this environment.

Rosie and Freddie relaxing at the foot of the Khumbu Icefall, looking back at the start of EBC, with a yak train arriving with supplies for climbing expeditions.

EBC NEPAL – DAYS 11-14

Back to Lukla

Heading back we tried to focus on the walk. Base Camp was now behind us but we still had a challenging 4 day walk back to Lukla. Our progress back was slower than what Ricky had hoped, so we had to stay an extra night in the Lobuche teahouse while the rest of the trekking staff took the Yaks to Periche for food and supplies. Ricky highlighted the issue using my map, we had really pushed the camping logistics to the limit by making a second attempt, meaning we had to split from the supporting staff for a day.

With an incredible walk behind them, it was time to remind ourselves that the kids were just 9 and 7 years old, and had achieved something remarkable. Chocolate was called for!

In Lobuche Ricky organised a special treat for the kids – a chocolate cake celebrating the achievement. We shared the cake with everyone in the teahouse, with a round of applause for Rosie and Freddie from the rest of the trekkers present.

Going downhill, we could relax more, noting that we were feeling much fitter and weren't feeling any altitude effects at all, which added to our mood.

On the way back to Lukla, the kids make a new friend "Pritzer".

Back in Thokla Rosie and Freddie were given a round of applause by an American group who had originally assumed that we were on our way uphill, possibly expecting us not to make it. "That's incredible", one said after hearing we had just been to base camp, "You guys are awesome parents!" As we continued downhill Rosie and Freddie went ahead, playing with a new found canine friend Pritzer, who they asked me to adopt. As we approached one of the stupas we heard joyous shouting and yelling.

Some more Americans approached us "Wow! You must be the parents! That's amazing – high five!" We didn't understand how they knew what we had done, Ricky and Kazi were behind us and wouldn't have advertised the fact, although Ricky had shared the achievement on Facebook. Had other guides on the mountain told their groups what we had done? We couldn't quite believe the purely positive response we were getting. Over the next couple of days we met many groups, I observed that those groups who were in

Polly gets to take a break from being behind the camera lens.

the middle of a challenging steep climb were much more muted and didn't respond overtly well, but not negatively, to seeing two kids. Groups which were on a rest break or relatively easy section we clearly far more outwardly positive and much more likely to interact or comment about the kids being on the trek route, an indicator that altitude really does affect the majority of people in some way. Without fail everyone who had heard that the kids had been to base camp was impressed. We heard later that as Freddie was clearly the youngest person on trek, one entire group used the sight of him keenly trekking uphill as a motivator. Before they saw him the adults in the group would occasionally complain about being tired and out of breath. After seeing him they would say to each other that if a seven year could do it so well, then they daren't complain and should get on with it!

Freddie feeling comfortable in his stride on the way downhill.

At Tengboche, we were blessed by a monk in the monastery. The ceremony started by us sitting cross-legged in one side of the temple. The monk, dressed in the red Tibetan gown, started chanting from a text, nodding his head backwards and forth towards us, with a giant statue of Buddha to the side. The deep tones created a very calming atmosphere. Myself and Polly were silent in respect, with Rosie and Freddie only just being patient enough to sit for the 15-minute experience.

The monastery at Tengboche.

Afterwards we stood up, to be presented with a narrow yellow string necklace, a blessing, which the monk tied around our neck, followed by placing his thumb on our foreheads. It was a very respectful and rewarding cultural experience. A blessing at Tengboche is usually reserved for mountaineers, for those who would be making a summit attempt, with it being seen as necessary for good luck and protection to ensure a safe journey. Ricky had kindly ensured that we experienced the custom as well. There is always something calming about Tibetan monasteries, the atmosphere is usually peaceful and respectful.

For comparison, when I had a blessing in Bangkok 15 years earlier, the local monk there was more wise to the tourist trade, so simply brushed some leaves at me, chanted a couple of sentences, and then complained when my tip wasn't big enough.

I also remembered that after our Tibetan trip, which had involved many monastery visits, my mind was as silent and peaceful as it had ever been, with no "mind gossip" at all going on. On returning to the UK from our Tibetan trip, as my workplace involved a commute on the M25, this feeling didn't last long. At the time I thought we should have Tibetan chants and bells at major road junctions back home, although I realised that it may cause some drivers to fall asleep!

One of the amusing observations on the trek was on the way back to Lukla, in the village of Kjangjuma, where we opted to camp outside a teahouse. The owner was very well known locally and had himself climbed Everest a couple of times. The teahouse was warm and welcoming inside, and a typical Nepalese focal point at night-time in the area, having a central yak-poo oven to gather around and socialise. While we were waiting for dinner, we watched one of the Transformer movies with other trekkers on their way uphill, which was a treat for the kids. The owner's wife sat beside me and we started to talk.

"Where are you from", she asked. I smiled at her.

"London", I replied.

"Ooooh, London, very good." She paused for a couple of seconds. "We've been there too". She then pointed to a framed photo of her and husband hanging on the wall in the corner, being embraced by Prince Charles at Buckingham Palace. "We enjoyed it very much, it's a very nice country". I tried not to laugh or react, but nodded in agreement that she had indeed experienced the typical London. I couldn't bear to tell her that not everyone got to have dinner with the Royal family. "Nepal is great too", I replied, wondering if she thought we all lived in mansions and lived across the road in a tight-knit community with the Windsors.

The next day our bodies started to creak! We were feeling the strain. I could really feel it on my shoulder and legs, I also realised that I may have fractured a big toe during martial arts training back home. All the rusty parts of my body were being exposed – I felt that I was getting old! No matter, I was instructed by Rosie to come and play volleyball with the crew outside the next teahouse, which was great fun at 3000m!

Freddie relaxing in the warmth of the sun before reaching Lukla.

As we descended, Freddie's sense of humour started to become clearer, perhaps the additional oxygen was putting him on a psychological high! He would continually take the mickey, a hereditary feature I've been told, and started collecting live ladybirds in his pocket. When he walked he'd try not to squash them, which slowed us down somewhat going downhill, but at least he was having fun!

On the way back to Lukla, Polly commented on the horsemanship being shown by one of the locals. A cowboy was calmly but efficiently navigating a horse down a flight of steep steps. He was on a traditional wooden saddle and was completely at ease with the situation. There was a symbiotic relationship between man and horse, something not often seen in the west.

Back towards Lukla near the park entrance we bought achievement certificates for the kids in a very basic hut at the side of the trail, to be framed back at home. Ricky asked if we wanted to stop for a drink in Lukla, and Polly mentioned something about Starbucks. Ricky said to me out of Polly's earshot that we could go for a beer while Polly and the kids go for coffee! I thought that as I was "the client" we should stick together and not split up like that. So, in the Irish Pub, Rosie strutted her stuff on the dancefloor as the adults enjoyed a well-deserved beer. I decided we'd give Starbucks a miss. We had the establishment to ourselves, this being 11am. We couldn't quite believe the sheer energy the kids still had, and I didn't realise Rosie had such good dance moves! I bought Kazi and Ricky a beer, we said cheers and thanks for the support. Later we had our last meal with the crew, I gave a thankyou speech on behalf of Polly and myself, and said that we hoped our story would inspire other trekkers to return to Nepal to experience what we had.

Back in Kathmandu we said goodbye to Ricky, Kazi and Syem, with the three of them adding to our most amazing trip yet. I thought EBC in Tibet was incredible, our experience here seemed one step higher, thanks to the fantastic support we had been given.

Everest Trekking With Kids

A photo with our trekking staff and additional family. Looking back, trekking with a crew does support many individuals directly, both locally and even back to Kathmandu, and we realised we could not have done our trip successfully without their support.

CHAPTER FIVE
Kathmandu, Camp Hope

At Dwarika's, we noted that the hotel was involved with charitable work, involved with the maintenance and planning of a project to return displaced earthquake victims back to the mountains, by building new earthquake-proof houses. The Dwarika's Foundation was created to raise US$5 million in order to create 6 new villages, with new houses costing $15,000 each. Each house would be built to a set engineering standard along with associated community buildings. The residents were already identified and were waiting in camps such as Camp Hope, a temporary tented village for 200 villagers, all displaced since April 2015. We decided to visit the village, as hotel guests are permitted to do, to see for ourselves how the project was progressing. On arrival the "village" seemed to be located in a suburb of Kathmandu, in quite a built-up area. The camp consisted of several dozen shacks, with some running water (through a single hosepipe), a single community kitchen, some workshops and a television area with old 14" TV. This was basic.

The camp population seemed happy with what they had, the recent addition of the single hose for running water was

Visiting Camp Hope, a charitable camp supported by Dwarika's hotel, housing displaced villagers in the aftermath of the Nepal earthquake.

a major achievement for them. We were shown around by a camp guide, a teenager who was very friendly and knew the workings of the camp inside out. Rosie and Freddie mixed well with the kids from the camp. We were shown around the workshop area, where basic products were made for sale, as well as school classroom and library with a small range of books. What struck us about the community there was that after being there for a year, they had made it a working home. Yes they were living off charity, but they were happy. They also knew and believed in the plan to resettle in a year or so after the new homes were built. The building process was delayed as we were told, the US and Nepalese geologists who were monitoring the proposed new village areas wanted to wait for another year, to ensure that the fresh earthquake-sourced landslides had settled after monsoonal conditions, ensuring it was a safe location to build on. To us this seemed very frustrating, but we could see the logic.

We appreciated the opportunity to visit Camp Hope, as it gave the kids a chance to see what work charities do on the ground. I personally felt that as a western visitor we were

We say our goodbyes, with our children mixing well with the camp children.

incredibly privileged, we could come from the UK, go the mountains at will, do our thing, go back to Kathmandu and then head home when we liked. Whereas these villagers had lost their mountain homes, had been forced to move to Kathmandu by circumstance, were basically living off handouts, and were not allowed to return to the mountains. Polly and I agreed that we could try to do more for people in that situation. This approach went hand-in-hand with our promotion of our kid's achievement in the Nepalese media. We were offered an interview with the Nepali Times and the hotel tried to arrange a Nepalese TV appearance for us, although we ran out of time for that. The Nepali Times sent a reporter around to the hotel to interview us. The reporter had only some knowledge of trekking and the mountains, but she and editor managed to put together a story to promote what we trying to achieve, showing off Nepal as a great destination for trekking, despite the recent earthquake. (See *"Trekking is Child's Play"*, Nepali Times 18th April 2016). At least we had achieved something in being the subject of this article, and hopefully have encouraged some trekkers to continue their plans for Nepal.

Meanwhile back in the UK, we assessed standards of British media reporting from Nepal as being inadequate. The typical comment projected an image of Kathmandu as being wrecked with no progress being made on repairing the damage, and with no comment on the condition of the rest of the country. We thought that an opportunity for positivity was being missed, how could a country known for its mountaineering be wrecked, yet British 7 and 9 year-old children had just completed its most significant trek? We shared our Nepal story with a few friends, who all reacted positively to what we had done.

Polly and I hope that the telling of this story would encourage others to challenge themselves and their kids, in a safe and responsible way. This book has been published to promote awareness of the Nepalese situation and also to highlight it as a truly great outdoor travel destination.

Trekking is child's play

YUWEI LIEW

Rosie and Freddie Mundell are among the youngest people in the world who can say they've been to both sides of Mt Everest. The young trekkers along with their parents had trekked to the northern Base Camp on the Tibetan side two years ago when they were just seven and six.

This month, the family returned to the base of world's highest mountain from the Nepal side (above) and made their way to advanced base camp at around 5500m. Parents Neil and Polly Mundell say their goal was not to make or break any records.

"It was just the right time for us to make this trip," said Polly. "Both of us have plenty of high-altitude experience, and we had a brilliant expedition team, which is why we felt safe bringing the kids up to Base Camp."

A penchant for scaling heights certainly seems to run in the family. The couple met in Ecuador while climbing Mt Cotopaxi and although their attempt to summit it was unsuccessful, the pair hit it off from there. Rosie and Freddie are clearly following their parents' footsteps when it comes to their love for the mountains.

From the children's point of view, the hardest part of the journey wasn't the physical demands or the altitude. "The scariest part was the flight to Lukla," said Rosie. "The plane just kept shaking and shaking."

The parents said their children handled the trek remarkably well, attributing their success to the preparation they had undergone. "We brought the kids up to Wales to do a lot of walking before we came over, and we made sure to teach them about earthquake safety," said Neil. "The first night we were here, we simulated an earthquake drill and got them to go the corners of the room with strong structural support."

Polly also stressed the importance of addressing the children's' fears beforehand.

"Because we had these conversations about earthquakes, they're not going to be as scared as they would be if something happens that they don't fully understand or expect."

Polly and Neil also hope the trip would allay any concerns of their friends that Nepal was unsafe to visit after the earthquake, and know many who had cancelled their Nepal treks. They say trekking tourism is the best way to help Nepal recover.

While weighing the risks of visiting Nepal a year after the earthquake, Neil, a geologist, explained that there was actually a lower risk of a big earthquake occurring again so soon.

"Once the tectonic tension is released after a big earthquake, you'll get aftershocks of smaller and smaller sizes. So the chances of having a second big earthquake are actually slimmer," he explained. But the couple acknowledged that while life has its risks, they would not be stopped by their fear of the unknown.

"We were very conscious of the reality of an earthquake. With Nepal's geological position, I think it's inevitable," said Polly. "But it's like the terrorism. You can't let these things scare you or put you off."

The achievement was published in the Nepali Times

APPENDIX – PREPARATION NOTES

'By failing to prepare, you are preparing to fail'
- Benjamin Franklin

In mid-late 2015 I decided to put pen to paper in part to manifest the intense and continual feeling of pride and jaw-dropping disbelief when recalling what my kids had achieved in Tibet. When researching equivalent achievements we realised that it really was very rare. Most treks to EBC described on the internet were naturally to Nepal, as travel is much more common there.

Before travelling to Tibet, we undertook a risk assessment and considered various "what-if?" scenarios. Travelling with kids is challenging under normal circumstances, but at high altitude in a remote area, camping in an under-developed part of the world, during a 70km trek with little support - would this be even possible? Our perceived and considered risks were clearly altitude sickness, evacuation plan in case of injury, isolation due to extreme weather and personal crime. Being both experienced trekkers, international travellers, as well as having the financial resources, meant we could address our concerns to some degree. Altitude sickness was the one primary concern that we could not predict; we had no guarantee that Polly's careful itinerary preparation (being familiar with Tibet) would prevent any one of us, particularly the kids, from suffering. My own logic was simple. There are millions of people in Tibet, therefore a lot of kids, and as kids are more adaptable than adults, the slow adjustment planned would be fine. My logic went further, that if we were suffering severely in relatively lower altitudes in Lhasa, we would pull the plug and not attempt the trek, which would be a hugely expensive decision.

We realized the potential risk of an earthquake, but we didn't take it seriously. I figured that even with a 1 in 20 year event, there was a less than one percent chance of us being in the region at the time. Less than a year after our trip, we would look at our Kathmandu photographs in particular at the many monuments with the kids playing on, now destroyed forever.

Regarding altitude sickness and adaptation in kids, we observed them being affected initially as I was, particularly in Lhasa, and then the familiar pattern of rapid recovery occurring which we normally see in our kids. Since they have smaller bodies they are susceptible to changes in the environment and feel them quickly, with the flip side in the positive case being very rapid recovery. Trying to get medical advice in the UK on issues such as Diamox for kids (which wasn't available, so we decided not to use it ourselves) was difficult. Even the internet had very few genuinely informative statements, this being a testament to how unusual our trip would be.

Of the many scare stories (many justifiable) we focused on those to EBC. I was shocked to read of individuals who would travel from low altitudes straight to Lhasa and then straight to EBC within just a couple of days, only to be found seriously ill or dead afterwards in their lodgings. My own experience tells me very clearly - you must go slowly. The common guidelines and rules of thumb I have heard from trekking staff, was to climb perhaps 300m per day, and sleep low to adjust when possible. In Ecuador in 2004 I experienced 12 hours of what I thought was altitude effects at the refuge at 4800m before attempting to summit Cotopaxi, concluding afterwards that my personal onset was above 4500m, whereas I definitely felt the altitude in Lhasa at 3650m. Despite travelling in Tibet for 3 weeks going to a maximum altitude of over 5300m, physically I was still becoming fitter and adjusting to the thinner air even at the end of the trip.

I previously suffered from malaria in 1998 and spent a week in hospital, being very seriously ill. Beforehand I considered myself to be very fit and easily capable of overcoming any illness. Over the following months I observed a staged initial recovery followed by a longer term return to fitness. Having been through that I have no issue in stating that even the fittest of people on paper can still succumb to seemingly random afflictions. Do not assume that just because you perceive yourself to be fit you will be fine at high altitude! Our advice to anyone travelling to high altitude making a rapid ascent, is not to, unless you have done it many times before and are surrounded by experienced people who can help.

Travelling in Nepal and Tibet in August also had the additional complication of the monsoon, especially in Nepal on the western flanks of the Tibetan plateau. When we arrived in Kathmandu the local trekking company told us that the Friendship Highway (our overland exit route from Tibet) had experienced a lot of landslides and heavy rainfall, so there was a chance that we would have to book a helicopter to extract us. I thought that as there were 3 weeks for repair work it may not be such an issue, but as events evolved several villages were swept away during our trip and the road became completely impassable. Polly, having been to Tibet before, was more concerned that the loss of the planned overland border crossing would mean there was a chance we would get stuck in Tibet for longer, as other border crossings were occasionally closed. Individuals opted to walk the route, risking other landslides over sheer drops. As we had kids we asked for a helicopter to return from the Tibetan border back to Kathmandu. Somehow our trekking company managed to find us some seats in the chaos, with the helicopter being arranged to pick us up from a 20m wide terrace on the side of a mountain on a makeshift landing pad. This resembled a military-style extraction rather than comfortable and safe family outing.

Despite the issues here there were many other minor inconveniences, and a strong element of "roughing it" at the campsites every night, despite all of the planning and generally good intentions of operators. Trekking to Everest Base Camp in Tibet was much more hazardous than we initially thought.

In 2016 for our Nepal trip our kids were clearly older, physically stronger with even stronger opinions. Freddie had developed his negotiating style, and for trekking to EBC in Nepal managed to extract the promise of a trip to Disneyland in Hong Kong! I wasn't present when the promise was made but was in no position to disagree!

In preparation for this next major trek, we again went through the kit list (see below), updated for growing kids, and had a few weekends in the Lake District and Snowdon. We had kept up a fitness regime over the winter so felt much fitter at the start of the Nepal trek compared to Tibet.

This trip was planned to be more condensed, a 17 day trip in total at Easter, with 12 days on trek. The major concerns this time were earthquakes (again not likely to occur during our short visit), altitude related illness, poor weather, injury and the world's most dangerous flight to contend with. Polly voiced concerns over the internal Nepal flight having narrowly avoided a fatal crash many years earlier on a flight from Pokhara to Jomsom. Her feeling wasn't helped by an employee of a local outdoor shop near our home, who also narrowly missed a different fatal plane crash in Nepal. I tried to convince her with statistics, that there were several thousand flights per year to Lukla, all of them safe bar one recent crash. So logically the risks were low. Then on February 23rd, around a month before our departure, a Tara Air flight crashed killing all 23 on board. Who were we booked on asked Polly – Tara Air. Again logic dictates that there was no reason to change airline, but as we had already been in contact with the UK national press, we may have been frowned upon for not taking this incident in account in our planning should the unlikely occur again. So we changed to Goma Air, who also flew to Lukla, a newer airline with a good safety record.

For this trip we undertook a thorough preparation and planning including:-

- 3 weekends of intensive walking in Wales and the Lake District
- Weekly long walks around London
- Polly and I undertook intensive gym sessions e.g. I used step machines to build up from 1250 steps to 2000 at between 60-90 steps per minute. This was equivalent to 90+ floors of a building, in other words I'd walk up the equivalent of The Shard after work!

The trek was over 60km each way, with our addition Lobuche-Gorak Shep duplication we trekked well over 120km in 14 days. We bought the highest quality outdoor equipment we could locate through specialist outdoor stores:- Cotswolds Outdoors, Adventure Peaks, Marmot and Little Trekkers of Ambleside. The minimum kit we used included (each):-

- 1 x pair of worn-in boots
- 3 pairs trekking socks
- 2 x trousers
- 2 x T-shirts (merino)
- 1 x fleece
- 1 x Pertex Primaloft jacket
- 1 x down jacket

- 1 x waterproof jacket
- 2 x hats
- 2 x sunglasses, one was Spectron-4 for highest altitudes
- Head torch with Energiser Lithium Ultimate batteries – good for cold weather (rated to minus 40 degrees C, but perhaps unnecessary for this trek?)

For reference, I slept in 1 x merino 260 Icebreaker, thermal leggings, 1 x Rab Ascent 900 sleeping bag (no liner), and a thin mattress was supplied.

Standard good quality DSLR batteries were fine, we didn't need cold weather lithium, just normal 2-3 lithium rechargeable for around 900 photos in my case. Polly used more batteries for more photos. You can recharge batteries in teahouses at cost (around £3 per charge, power banks usually not allowed). I took an Anker 20,000mAh battery pack which retained its power well and managed several Canon DSLR battery charges from it using a USB charger easily found on eBay. I also took an Anker 15W solar panel, and occasionally used it to charge the Canon DSLR batteries directly via USB connection. Ricky also charged his mobile phone directly from it simultaneously. Cost-wise solar panels do not make sense on this trek unless you are always camping away from teahouses for more than a week, or have addition use for them later.

Physical training wise, I lost 1 stone on trek. Walking with a backpack in Wales was useful, especially adding a few heavy rocks to bulk-out my bag to 15kg.

Running/step machines were ok but the risk of pulling

tendons meant it was sensible to stop this type of training one week before departure. I only managed 1x10km road run in the 3 months prior, 5-6 x 5km gym runs on the treadmill, usually with inclines thrown in, 5 x 1000-2000 steps on the step machine in the prior 6 weeks. Note with the step machine, the pace was 60-90 steps per minute, whereas in reality trekking is slow to very slow. During some steep climbs at high altitude the pace was as slow as 10-15 steps per minute. Beware that fast pace training may result in a desire to go faster when on trek – not a good idea!

As a guide I could easily do 40-50 press-ups. Looking back I could have done more work carrying a backpack, the average trek day was 6-9 hours, carrying 10kg along with a 3kg camera bag.

Altitude – beneficial to go slow, be as slow as you can reasonably get away with, avoiding walking in the dark! On the rest-day at Dingboche we had a practice 300m climb as part of our acclimatisation. As it was steep I used an altimeter to promise the kids that we'd give them a break every 50m to make sure they wouldn't have sore heads, and to ration their sweet supply! This had the effect of imposing a break on all of us every 10 minutes or so, for a rest and drinking session. This felt unnatural to do, as instinctively from fitness training there is a desire to "feel" as if we are pushing our bodies, whereas we were going slowly and also taking lots of breaks. Having the kids with us was an asset in this regard as their pace meant we simply couldn't push faster, which had the effect of allowing us to acclimatise more effectively. During this walk it was all too easy to be tempted to become frustrated at the slow pace, but luckily the views were amazing so Polly also encouraged us to go slow by talking lots of photos, and I took some video.

On a later walk from Lobuche-Gorak Shep Freddie dictated the timing of water breaks as he was suffering with a sore head. I observed that he naturally asked for a break almost exactly every 25m altitude gain, no matter what the grade of the slope was. We drank lots of water with him, and by the time we arrived in Gorak Shep (4 hours later rather than the typical 3) any initial headaches in our group had gone completely and we were well hydrated despite us increasing our altitude – a brilliant result! This section of trek demonstrated that going slow (lots of breaks plus an almost tediously slow pace) as well as drinking lots of water (over 2 litres in 4 hours in my case, air temperature maybe 15 degrees C) combated altitude effects and improved our altitude performance compared to the previous day. Pace on the steepest sections was perhaps one step every 3-5 seconds. This may seem slow but we only needed to climb 300m in a few hours (100m per hour equates to 1.5m per minute, equivalent to around only six steps on a step machine per minute – I don't recommend you do this in a gym, you will get some strange looks!)

Early in our trek, we shared part of the route with a large travel group. The group would typically go off ahead of us at a faster pace, and then need much longer rests than us (they'd actually watch us catch up and walk past them time after time), so in the end their overall pace was similar. However, as their actual walking pace was faster when moving, being young adults, their exertion overall would have been higher i.e. they spent more time in the higher heart-rate zone. Not all of the group made it, with numerous cases of AMS developing later in the trek. Perhaps if they had tempered the more ambitious individuals within the group and maintained a slower pace, more of them may have made it, and they would have required less rest time. I observed that when comparing trekking groups made up of initial strangers, the culture of the group is dictated by the "leaders" who then influenced the others. Where is the Nepalese guide you may ask? They are clearly present, but as they themselves are already acclimatised and used to people "not being suited to altitude" they may have a tendency to accept a faster pace and therefore accept a needlessly higher drop-out rate due to altitude sickness. A different approach is possible, and adopted by some guides – one where the trek leaders deliberately stop the faster individuals from influencing the rest of the group, and let the slow members dictate the pace as long as the daily target is met in a reasonable time.

The benefit of a private trip is that Polly and I were the clients, so we dictated the pace (to suit the kids). Within our trek team we had a trek leader/guide Ricky as well as a Sherpa Kazi. Kazi was very good at setting a slow pace – although we asked him on occasions to go even slower if we observed that the kids, who were usually well behind him, would have benefited from it. Previous treks we have been on did not include a pace-setter, only a guide who tends to be more schedule orientated. Having a formal pace-setter may therefore be a good idea for inexperienced trekkers or those groups who may have more impatient members.

In attempting to summarise our observations regarding altitude effects, I was unable to locate any diagram online which could explain the importance of self-monitoring in relation to walking pace. This is a key aspect of avoiding and reducing the risk of AMS, and one which a pictorial representation might clarify why walking pace is important in safe trekking. The basic concept in reducing AMS risk is to minimise the total effort made while making progress at gaining new altitude highs (refer to figure). There is an inherent contradiction in *making an effort* to walk uphill while trying to acclimatise, which can manifest as AMS if the correct balance is not struck. The aim of the diagram is not to attempt to add to existing more research-based scientific knowledge, but merely to summarise observations to the lay person what the main issue is when undertaking high altitude treks. Consider the three situations (1-3, labelled).

The figure is split into two sections A (top) and B (bottom). Section A refers to the heart rate and climb rate which are generally linked. Section B applies to those trekkers who are not fully acclimatised to the new altitude. Going at a slow pace (1), the trekker will experience low heart-rates in the green "non-exertion" range. As pace increases (2 and 3), so does heart-rate. To the fully acclimatised person this is not an issue. The Y-axis has been labelled as Acclimatising Poorly (increased risk of AMS) towards the top and Acclimatising Well towards the X-axis. A notional threshold "Altitude Deficit Line", related to exertion is used to demonstrate when the body may start to struggle with what is being asked of it. Moderate (2) and fast (3) paces are shown to be above the Altitude Deficit Line, meaning (see right hand Y-axis) that there is an increased requirement for time spent resting, and therefore a corresponding increased risk of AMS. There will also be a time element to this concept, with more time spent at a faster pace also increasing the rest time requirement and risk of AMS. Individual reactions to trekking at different paces will depend on many factors, but in general pace effects everybody's reaction to altitude.

After many observations of trekkers, and our own experience, I would emphasise that time (especially at a fast pace) spent above the "Altitude Deficit Line" creates a cumulative effect of an increasing requirement to rest. Time spent at a faster pace at altitude increases the risk of AMS. Taking more rest times during trekking, in order to justify a fast walking pace, may therefore be more counterproductive than simply maintaining a slow and steady pace.

Put simply, the figure visually shows that a slower pace helps with acclimatisation.

Everest Trekking With Kids

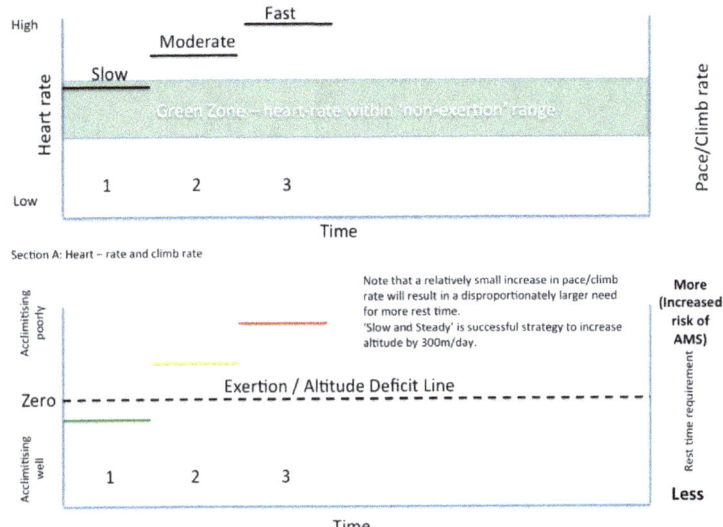

A figure to highlight our views on acclimatisation. As pace increases from 1 to 2 to 3, so does the likelihood of physical exertion on the body. In unacclimatised individuals an "Altitude Deficit" and corresponding rest-time requirement accumulates, which may lead to AMS symptoms. Going slow and avoiding over-exertion, even brief periods of over exertion, helps to reduce the risk of illness.

ABOUT THE AUTHOR

Neil Mundell was born in Larne, Northern Ireland. He studied geology at Aberdeen University, Scotland before starting his career in the oil & gas industry. Several years of working around the world developed his understanding and respect of other cultures. Later, he moved to London to do a masters degree at Imperial College London, and continued the search for new oil & gas. A natural explorer in many ways, he also has a keen interest in cultural influences on behaviour, ethics and people development.

Polly Mundell was born in Swindon, England, the daughter of a headmaster in a family of geography teachers. She followed in her family's footsteps but rebelled by focusing on English Literature. A Cambridge University graduate, and enormously well read in Indian literature, she travels at every opportunity to interact with different cultures, and loves to take the time to observe and frame every scene through her passion for photography. She has a natural love of people and trekking in the third world.

Neil and Polly met in Ecuador under Quito's statue of an angel, before trekking in the Andes. They became closer on the trip and were ultimately tethered together by rope when climbing Cotopaxi. Since then they have had two children who accompany them on adventures throughout the world.

Prior to visiting Tibet, the couple had a plan to introduce Yak-butter tea into high-class grocery stores in the UK – but have since decided not to.

www.ingramcontent.com/pod-product-compliance
Lightning Source LLC
Chambersburg PA
CBHW070106080526
44586CB00013B/1206